MW00785486

Contents

Math Strand Colors

- Number and Operations
- Algebra
- Geometry
- Measurement
- Data Analysis and Probability
- Problem Solving

Ready-Made Centers
for Differentiated Instruction

① Each of the 5 spiral-bound books in the box contains an on-level, one-star activity, and an advanced-level, two-star activity, for every lesson.

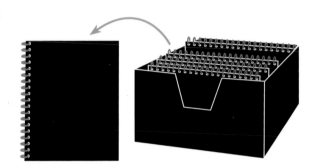

One-star activity

Two-star activity

② Manipulatives

20 number cubes

100 red and 100 blue square tiles

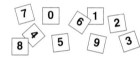

10 sets of number tiles (0-9)

③ Plastic Bags:

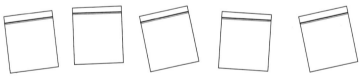

5 plastic bags

④ School-supplied items:

20 large paper clips

35 small paper clips

5 paper lunch bags

Divide all materials equally into the 5 plastic bags.

20 red square tiles

20 blue square tiles

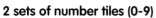

2 sets of number tiles (0-9)

7 small paper clips

4 large paper clips

4 number cubes

 Store the activity materials in the front section of the box.

- Each group of students doing an activity grabs a book, a plastic bag of manipulatives, and (if needed) a paper bag. Groups then work independently to complete one or both leveled activities.

- Occasionally, manipulatives and/or Teaching Tool masters used during the lesson will also be needed to complete the Center Activities.

- When students complete an activity, they return the book and the bag of manipulatives to the box.

Play a Game

Partner Talk
Share your thinking while you work.

Start Put ⬜1 ⬜2 ⬜3 ⬜4 ⬜5 ⬜6 ⬜7 ⬜8 ⬜9 in a .

Get 18 red squares. Give one game board to each player.
Play at the same time.

Try Pick a tile. Look at the number. What if that number of ducks
joined these ducks? How many ducks would there be?
Say an addition sentence with the number in all.
If you see the sum on your game board, cover it.
Put the tile aside. Repeat until one player wins.

Four Corners

14	8	13
15	10	7
9	12	11

Four Corners

11	14	10
15	7	9
8	13	12

To win, be the first player to cover four corners.

Try Again Play again!

Play a Game

Partner Talk

Share your thinking while you work.

Start 🤸 Put  0 1 2 3 4 5 6 7 8 9 in a 🛍.

Get 18 red squares. Give one game board to each player.
Play at the same time.

Try Pick a tile. Look at the number. What if that number of ducks joined these ducks? How many ducks would there be?
Say an addition sentence with the number in all.
If you see the sum on your game board, cover it.
Put the tile aside. Repeat until one player wins.

Four Corners

13	10	15
16	8	12
11	14	17

Four Corners

17	11	14
13	8	15
16	9	12

To win, be the first player to cover four corners.

Try Again Play again!

Try Together

Partner Talk
Share your thinking while you work.

Start 🏃 Put ①②③④⑤⑥⑦⑧⑨ in a 🛍 .

Get 9 red squares. Take turns.

Try Pick a tile. Put that number of red squares on the other part of the mat. Ask your partner to say an addition sentence to find the number of squares in all.

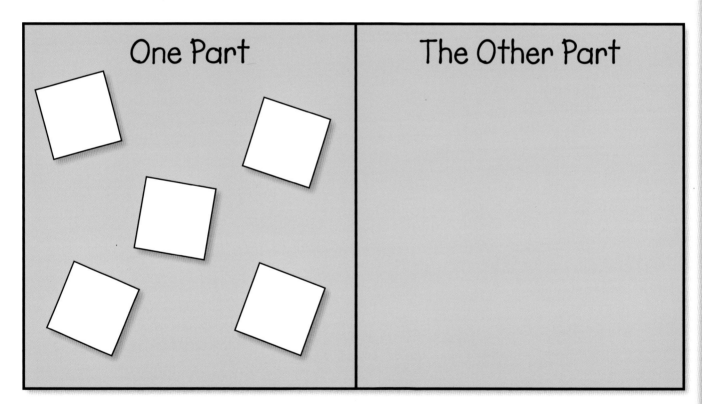

One Part	The Other Part

Say: "5 plus _____ equals _____."

Put the tile aside. Remove your squares. Repeat until the 🛍 is empty.

Try Again Put the tiles back in the 🛍 . Repeat the activity. Talk about how joining two parts helps you to find the number of squares on the whole mat.

Try Together

Start 👥 Put 0 1 2 3 4 5 6 7 8 9 in a 🛍️.

Get 9 red squares. Take turns.

Try Pick a tile. Put that number of red squares on the other part of the mat. Ask your partner to say an addition sentence to find the number of squares in all.

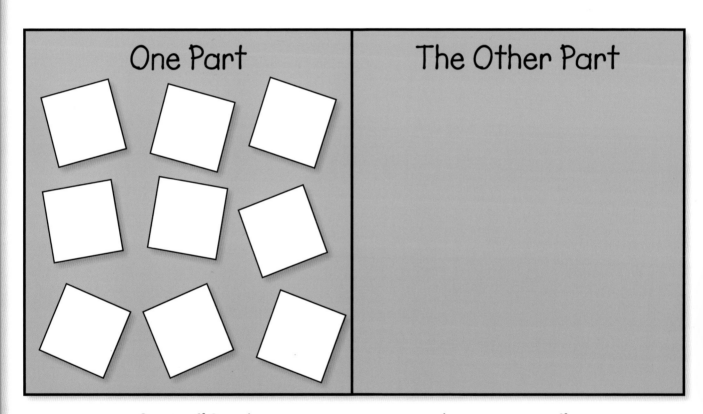

One Part	The Other Part

Say: "9 plus _____ equals _____."

Put the tile aside. Remove your squares. Repeat until the 🛍️ is empty.

Try Again Put the tiles back in the 🛍️. Repeat the activity. Tell how this activity could be like making a paper chain.

Helping Hands

Partner Talk
Share your thinking while you work.

Start Put  in a . Take turns.

Try Pick a tile to show how many seeds you will take out of the seed packet. Use your fingers to show how many seeds will be left in the seed packet.

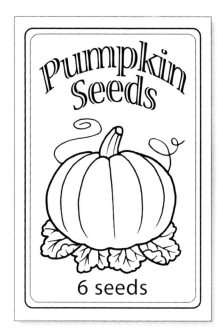

Pumpkin Seeds

6 seeds

Ask your partner to say a subtraction sentence for your story.

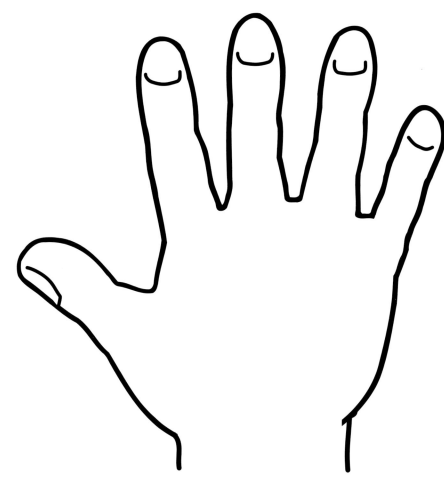

Put the tile aside. Repeat until the  is empty.

Try Again Put the tiles back the  . Repeat the activity.
Talk about taking things out of other kinds of packages.

Helping Hands

Partner Talk
Share your thinking while you work.

Start Put [2] [3] [4] [5] [6] [7] [8] [9] in a . Take turns.

Try Pick a tile to show how many seeds you will take out of the seed packet. Use your fingers to show how many seeds will be left in the seed packet.

Flower Seeds

12 seeds

Ask your partner to say a subtraction sentence for your story.

Put the tile aside. Repeat until the 🛍 is empty.

Try Again Put the tiles back in the 🛍. Repeat the activity. How is this activity like taking some eggs out of a carton that has a dozen eggs?

Look and See

Start 👥 Get a 🎲.
Get 6 red squares. Take turns.

Try Toss the cube to see how many birds will fly away.
Use the red squares to cover those birds.

Say: "_____ minus _____ equals _____."

Remove the squares. Repeat until each player gets 4 turns.

Try Again Take turns. Tell a separating story about 12 sea gulls on a beach. Ask your partner to tell how many are left.

Center Activity 1-4 ★

Topic 1   **7**

Look and See

Start 🏃 Get 🎲 🎲.
Get 12 red squares. Take turns.

Try Toss the 🎲 🎲. Add the numbers to see how many birds will fly away. Use red squares to cover that number of birds. Say the subtraction sentence for your story.

Say: "_____ minus _____ equals _____ ."

Remove the squares. Repeat until each player gets 4 turns.

Try Again Take turns. Tell a separating story about 18 sea gulls on a beach. Ask your partner to tell you how many are left.

Center Activity 1-4 ⭐⭐

Center Activity 1-5

 Put 6 blue squares and 6 red squares in a . Take turns.

 Take a handful of squares.
Separate them by color.
Put them in the spaces below.

Ask your partner to say a subtraction sentence
to compare the two rows of squares.

One color

The other color

Say: "_____ minus _____ equals _____."

Put your squares back in the bag.
Repeat until each player gets 4 turns.

Try Again Talk about some other things we compare in our world.

Center Activity 1-5 ⭐ Topic 1 **9**

Partner Talk

Share your thinking while you work.

Start Put 6 7 8 in a 🛍.

Get a 🎲. Get 8 blue squares. Get 6 red squares. Take turns.

Try Pick a tile. Place that many blue squares in the first row. Ask your partner to toss the number cube and put that many red squares in the second row. Say a subtraction sentence to compare the two rows of squares.

Blue Squares

Red Squares

Say: "_____ minus _____ equals _____."

Remove the squares. Put your tile back in the 🛍. Repeat until each player gets 4 turns.

Try Again If each row has the same number of squares, what happens when you compare those numbers?

Start  Get 12 red squares.
Cover each game space with a square.
Take turns.

Try Uncover two game spaces.

If you find one addition fact and two subtraction facts that have the same three numbers, keep the squares.

If not, put the squares back where they were.

Take turns until all the spaces are uncovered.

Memory Match

$6 + 5 = 11$	$14 - 8 = 6$ $14 - 6 = 8$	$5 + 7 = 12$	$13 - 8 = 5$ $13 - 5 = 8$
$15 - 6 = 9$ $15 - 9 = 6$	$12 - 7 = 5$ $12 - 5 = 7$	$11 - 5 = 6$ $11 - 6 = 5$	$5 + 8 = 13$
$4 + 6 = 10$	$9 + 6 = 15$	$10 - 6 = 4$ $10 - 4 = 6$	$6 + 8 = 14$

To win, collect the most squares.

Try Again Play again!

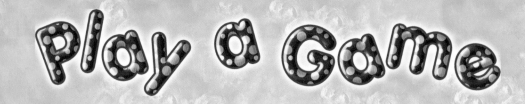

Partner Talk
Share your thinking while you work.

Start 🚶 Get 12 red squares.
Cover each game space with a square.
Take turns.

Try Uncover three game spaces.

If you see one addition fact and two subtraction facts that have the same numbers, keep the three squares.

If not, put the squares back where they were.

Take turns until all the spaces are uncovered.

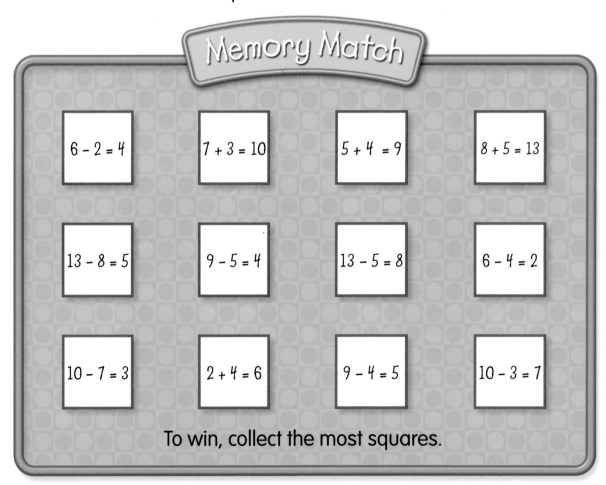

Memory Match

6 − 2 = 4	7 + 3 = 10	5 + 4 = 9	8 + 5 = 13
13 − 8 = 5	9 − 5 = 4	13 − 5 = 8	6 − 4 = 2
10 − 7 = 3	2 + 4 = 6	9 − 4 = 5	10 − 3 = 7

To win, collect the most squares.

Try Again Play again!

Partner Talk

Share your thinking while you work.

Start Get 9 red squares. Work together. Try every story.

Try Read a story to each other. Decide whether to add or subtract.
Use squares to help you solve the problem.
Find the matching number sentence. Read it together.

Sue had 8 marbles in her bag.
The bag had a hole in it and
4 marbles fell out.
How many marbles does
Sue have now?

Fred gave his teacher 3 flowers
this morning. Carly also brought
her teacher 4 flowers.
How many flowers does the
teacher have now?

Joey drew 7 butterflies
on his picture.
Then he drew 5 ladybugs.
How many more butterflies than
ladybugs did he draw?

6 apples fell off the apple tree.
3 more fell off the next day.
How many apples fell
off the tree altogether?

$4 + 4 = 8$

$8 - 4 = 4$

$6 - 3 = 3$

$7 - 5 = 2$

$6 + 3 = 9$

$3 + 4 = 7$

$4 - 3 = 1$

$7 - 2 = 5$

Try Again Take turns. Point to a number sentence.
Ask your partner to tell a story with those numbers.

Try Together

Partner Talk
Share your thinking while you work.

Start 👤 Get

Work together. Try every story.

Try Read a story to each other.
Use tiles to make an addition fact or a subtraction fact for that story.

> Annie carries 3 books to school.
> Jeannie carries
> 5 books to school.
> How many books do they
> carry altogether?

> Mike has 9 pennies in his bank.
> Rick has 7 pennies in his bank.
> How many more pennies
> does Mike have than Rick?

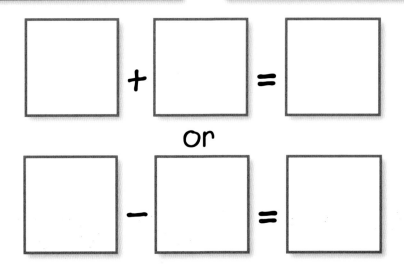

☐ + ☐ = ☐

or

☐ − ☐ = ☐

> There are 4 soccer balls
> in the basket.
> There are 5 footballs
> in the basket.
> How many balls are in the basket?

> 8 birds were perched
> on the tree.
> 2 birds flew away.
> How many birds are
> still in the tree?

Try Again Take turns. Make your own number sentence with tiles.
Ask your partner to tell you a story with those numbers.

Try Together

Start Put  in a .

Take turns.

Try Pick a tile. Place it in a square to show the missing answer.

Repeat until the is empty.

$$\begin{array}{r} 0 \\ + 2 \\ \hline \end{array}$$

$$\begin{array}{r} 2 \\ + 5 \\ \hline \end{array}$$

$$\begin{array}{r} 1 \\ + 0 \\ \hline \end{array}$$

$$\begin{array}{r} 2 \\ + 1 \\ \hline \end{array}$$

$0 + 0 =$

$2 + 7 =$

$6 + 2 =$

$4 + 2 =$

$1 + 3 =$

$5 + 0 =$

Try Again Put the tiles back in the . Take turns again.

Center Activity 2-1 ⭐

Topic 2   1

Try Together

Partner Talk

Share your thinking while you work.

Start 👥 Put 0 1 2 3 4 5 6 7 8 9 in a .

Take turns.

Try Pick a tile. Place it in a square to show the missing number.

Repeat until the is empty.

```
    3
  ┌───┐
+ │   │
  └───┘
    5
```

```
  ┌───────┐
  │       │
  │       │
  └───────┘
   + 6
  ─────────
     7
```

```
  ┌───────┐
  │       │
  │       │
  └───────┘
   + 8
  ─────────
     8
```

```
    2
  ┌───────┐
  │       │
+ │       │
  └───────┘
     7
```

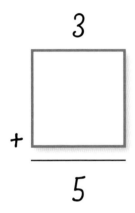 + 1 = 9

2 + ☐ = 5

2 + ☐ = 11

☐ + 2 = 8

☐ + 0 = 4

2 + ☐ = 9

Try Again Put the tiles back in the 🛍. Take turns again.

Cover Three

 Put  in a .

Get 10 red squares for one player. Get 10 blue squares for the other player. Take turns.

Try Pick a tile. Find one row of fish with that number.
Explain how to double your number. Cover the answer.
If the answer is taken, lose your turn. Put the tiles back in the 🛍.

10	8	2	6
12	14	18	14
18	16	0	8
8	4	12	16

To win, be the first player who gets squares in 3 connected game spaces. Look for these ways to win.

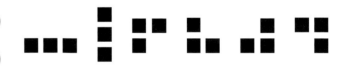

Try Again Play again!

Cover Three

Share your thinking while you work.

Start 👫 Get 🎲 🎲.
Get 10 red squares for one player. Get 10 blue squares for the other player. Take turns.

Try Toss 🎲 and 🎲. Count the dots. Follow directions.

Toss	Cover a space on the game board that shows a way to get this number in all.
2 dots	0
3 dots	2
4 dots	4
5 dots	6
6 dots	8
7 dots	10
8 dots	12
9 dots	14
10 dots	16
11 dots	18
12 dots	Lose your turn.

8 + 8	4 + 4	6 + 6	5 + 5
2 + 2	8 + 8	9 + 9	1 + 1
7 + 7	0 + 0	6 + 6	7 + 7
9 + 9	5 + 5	4 + 4	3 + 3

To win, be the first player who gets squares in 3 connected game spaces. Look for these ways to win.

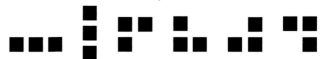

Try Again Play again!

Cover Three

Partner Talk
Share your thinking while you work.

Start Put   in a 🛍️.

Get 10 red squares for one player. Get 10 blue squares for the other player. Take turns.

Try Pick a tile. Find a school of fish that has that number and the next number. Explain how to add that number and the next number. Cover the answer. If the answer is taken, lose your turn. Put the tile back in the 🛍️.

11	5	17	3
13	15	7	9
17	3	13	15
9	11	7	5

To win, be the first player who gets squares in 3 connected game spaces. Look for these ways to win.

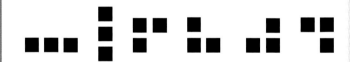

Try Again Play the game again!

Cover Three

Partner Talk

Share your thinking while you work.

Start  Get [dice].

Get 10 red squares for one player. Get 10 blue squares for the other player. Take turns.

Try Toss [dice]. Count the dots. Follow directions.

Toss	Cover a space on the game board that shows a way to get this number in all.
2 dots	Lose your turn.
3 dots	3
4 dots	5
5 dots	7
6 dots	9
7 dots	11
8 dots	13
9 dots	15
10 dots	17
11 dots	Lose your turn.
12 dots	Lose your turn.

2 +1	5 +6	4 +5	3 +4
7 +8	3 +2	6 +7	9 +8
4 +3	8 +9	1 +2	6 +5
7 +6	5 +4	8 +7	2 +3

To win, be the first player who gets squares in 3 connected game spaces. Look for these ways to win.

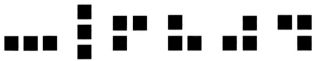

Try Again Play again!

Math in Motion

Partner Talk

Share your thinking while you work.

Start 🚶 Stand or sit next to your partner. Take turns.

Try

STEP 1 Hold up a different number of fingers on each hand.

Say the addition fact.

$5 + 2 = 7$

STEP 2 Cross one arm over the other.

Say the turn-around fact.

$2 + 5 = 7$

STEP 3 Ask your partner to repeat what you did and said.

Try Again Keep practicing!

Math in Motion

Partner Talk

Share your thinking while you work.

Start  Put ⑤ ⑥ ⑦ ⑧ ⑨ in a 🛍. Take turns.

Try

STEP 1 Pick a tile.

Show that number of fingers in all.

Hold up a different number of fingers on each hand.

Say the addition fact.

$5 + 3 = 8$

STEP 2

$3 + 5 = 8$

Cross one arm over the other.

Say the turn-around fact.

STEP 3 Ask your partner to show the same number in all with different turn-around facts.

Try Again Repeat until the is empty. Try again.

Center Activity 2-4 ★ ★

Partner Talk
Share your thinking while you work.

Try Together

Start  Put  in a 🛍️ .

Take turns.

Try 1. Pick 3 tiles.

2. Display the tiles in any order.

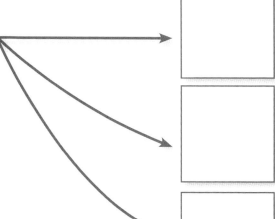

3. Explain how to add.
Point to the numbers you will add first.

4. Ask your partner to add in a different way.

5. Put the same tiles in any order here:

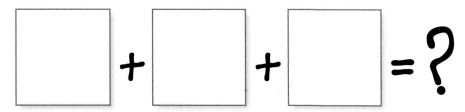

6. Repeat steps 3 and 4.

Try Again Put the tiles back in the 🛍️. Pick 3 tiles. Practice again.

Try Together

Partner Talk
Share your thinking while you work.

Start 👫 Put ⓪ ① ② ③ ④ ⑤ ⑥ ⑦ ⑧ ⑨ in a .

Take turns.

Try 1. Pick 3 tiles.

2. Display the tiles in any order.

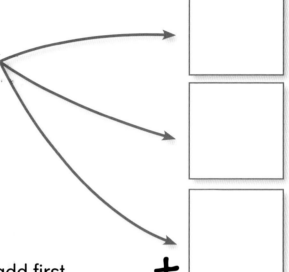

3. Explain how to add.
Point to the numbers you will add first.

4. Ask your partner to find two more ways
to add the three numbers.

5. Put the same tiles in any order here:

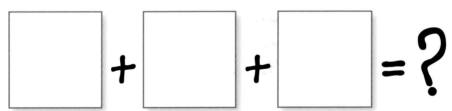

6. Repeat steps 3 and 4.

Try Again Put the tiles back in the 🛍. Pick 3 tiles. Practice again.

Helping Hands

Share your thinking while you work.

Start 🧍 or 🧍‍🧍 Put 1 2 3 4 5 6 7 8 9 in a .

Get 10 red squares. Get 10 blue squares.

Try

1. Show 9 people on the top level of the bus.

2. Pick a tile. Show that number of riders on the bottom.

3. Which numbers will you add to find the number of riders in all?

4. Explain how to make a 10 to add 9: Move one rider to the top level.

5. How many riders are there on the bus?

Try Again Repeat until the is empty. Begin again.

Helping Hands

Partner Talk

Share your thinking while you work.

Start 👤 or 👥 Put 1 2 3 4 5 6 7 8 in a .

Get 10 red squares. Get 10 blue squares.

Try 1. Show 10 people on the top level of the bus.

2. Pick a tile. Show that number of riders on the bottom. How many riders are there in all?

3. What if one person moves from the top to the bottom? Show what happens.

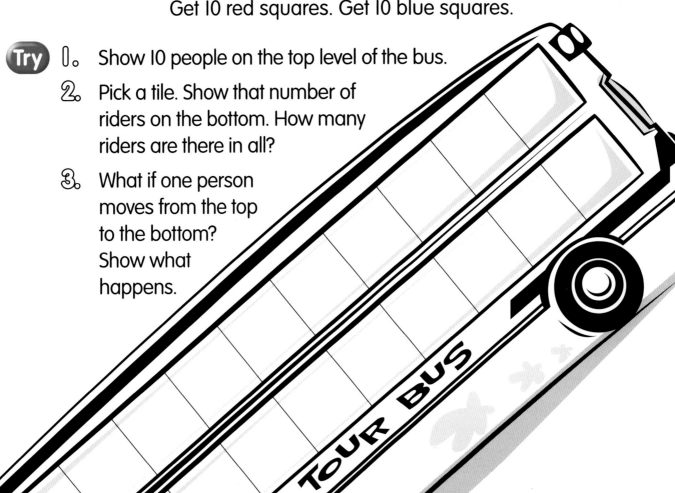

TOUR BUS

4. Say the addition fact, and a fact that shows the addends in a different order for the number of riders on both levels.

Try Again Repeat until the is empty. Begin again.

12 Topic 2   **Center Activity 2-6** ⭐ ⭐

Helping Hands

Start 👤 or 👥 Put [2] [3] [4] [5] [6] [7] [8] [9] in a 🛍️ .

Get 10 red squares. Get 10 blue squares.

Try

1. Show 8 people on the top level of the bus.

2. Pick a tile. Show that number of riders on the bottom.

3. Which numbers will you add to find the number of riders in all?

4. Explain how to make a 10 to add 8: Move two riders to the top level.

5. How many riders do you have on the bus?

Try Again Repeat until the 🛍️ is empty. Begin again.

Helping Hands

Share your thinking while you work.

Start 👤 or 👥 Put 2 3 4 5 6 7 in a 🛍.

Get 10 red squares. Get 10 blue squares.

Try

1. Show 10 people on the top level of the bus.

2. Pick a tile. Show that number of riders on the bottom. How many riders are there in all?

3. What if two people move from the top to the bottom? Show what happens.

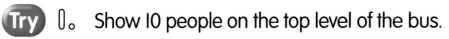

4. Say the addition fact, and a fact that shows the addends in a different order for the number of riders on both levels.

Try Again Repeat until the 🛍 is empty. Begin again.

Try Together

Partner Talk

Share your thinking while you work.

Start  Get 0 1 2 3 4 5 6 7 8 9 and 0 1 2 3 4 5 6 7 8 9 .

Work together. Read the table.
Talk about what the table tells you.

Try Read a question. Say a number sentence to solve the problem. Then use tiles to answer the question.

Push-ups in Gym Class

	Week 1	Week 2	Week 3
Billy	6	7	6
Cathy	3	5	5
Chris	4	4	5

1. How many push-ups did the children do in Week 1?

2. How many push-ups did Chris do in Week 2 and Week 3?

3. Look at Week 3. Use doubles or doubles plus one to tell how many push-ups the children did in all.

Try Again Take turns. Make up your own questions about the numbers in the table. Ask your partner to show the answer with number tiles.

Try Together

Start Get

0 1 2 3 4 5 6 7 8 9

and 0 1 2 3 4 5 6 7 8 9 .

Work together. Read the tables.
Talk about what the tables tell you.

Try Read a question.
Say a number sentence to solve the problem.
Then use the tiles to answer the question.

1. How many books were overdue on Monday?

2. How many overdue books did Grade 2 have on all three days?

Overdue Library Books

	Monday	Tuesday	Wednesday
Grade 1	1	0	2
Grade 2	3	1	4
Grade 3	2	2	1

3. How many overdue books did Grade 3 have on Monday and Wednesday?

Answer all your questions here.
Use number tiles.

Collection of Autumn Leaves

	Orange	Red	Brown
Sally	9	2	6
Fred	6	7	6
Cameron	8	4	5

4. How many leaves did Fred collect?

5. How many red leaves and orange leaves did Cameron collect?

Try Again Take turns. Make up your own question about the numbers in a table. Ask your partner to show the answer with number tiles.

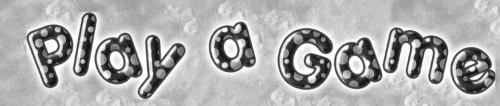

Partner Talk

Share your thinking while you work.

Start 👥 Get 20 red squares for one player.
Get 20 blue squares for the other player.

Put [0] [1] [2] in a 🛍️. Take turns.

Try Point to and say a number next to the game board. Pick a tile.
Follow directions in the rectangle below. Then put the tile back in the 🛍️.

IF YOU EXPLAIN HOW TO FIND	COVER
[0] less than your number	
[1] less than your number	
[2] less than your number	

Start Here!

Cover the Path!

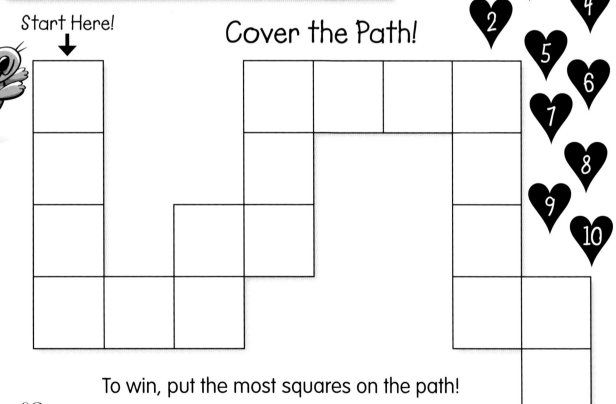

To win, put the most squares on the path!

Try Again Play again!

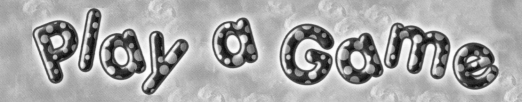 **Play a Game**

Partner Talk
Share your thinking while you work.

Start  Put 0 1 2 in a bag.

Get 20 red squares for one player. Get 20 blue squares for the other player. Get 🎲 🎲. Take turns.

Try Toss the 🎲 🎲. Pick a tile.
Follow directions.
Put the tile back in the bag.

EXPLAIN HOW TO FIND	COVER
0 less than the number you tossed	⬜
1 less than the number you tossed	⬜ ⬜
2 less than the number you tossed	⬜ ⬜ ⬜

Start Here!
↓

Cover the Path!

To win, put the most squares on the path!

Try Again Play again!

Look and See

Start Get 9 red squares. Take turns.

Try Point to a caterpillar and explain how to double that number. Say the addition sentence for your double. Ask your partner to look for the related subtraction fact on a leaf. Have your partner say the subtraction sentence and put a square on that leaf.

Repeat until all the leaves are covered.

Try Again Remove the squares. Repeat the activity.

★ ★ ★

Look and See

Partner Talk

Share your thinking while you work.

Start 👥 Put  1 1 2 2 3 3 4 4 5 5 6 6 7 7 8 8 9 9 in a 🛍.

Get 18 red squares. Take turns.

Try Pick a tile. Make and say a doubles fact with that number. Find a related subtraction fact for your doubles fact. Put a square on it. Play until the 🛍 is empty.

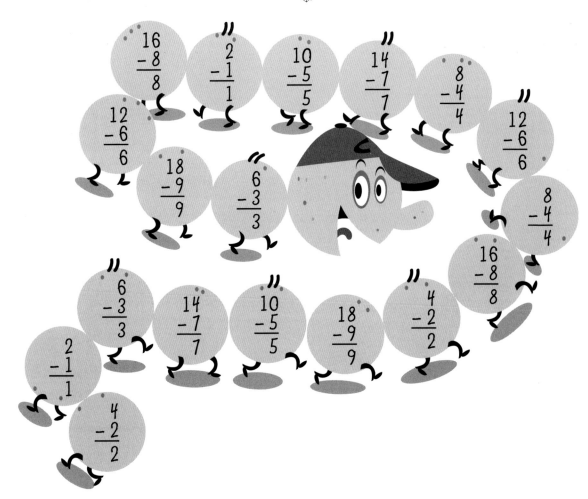

Try Again Say a doubles fact that has the number of body circles on the caterpillar. Remove the squares. Play again.

Play a Game

Start 🏃 Put 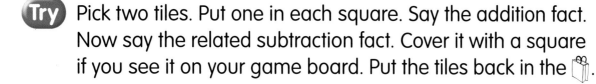 0 1 2 3 4 5 in a 🛍.

Get 18 red squares.
Give one game board to each player. Take turns.

Try Pick two tiles. Put one in each square. Say the addition fact. Now say the related subtraction fact. Cover it with a square if you see it on your game board. Put the tiles back in the 🛍.

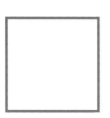 **+**  **=** ____

Win with Five

1 − 0 ⎯⎯ 1	6 − 4 ⎯⎯ 2	3 − 0 ⎯⎯ 3
6 − 1 ⎯⎯ 5	5 − 2 ⎯⎯ 3	7 − 5 ⎯⎯ 2
7 − 3 ⎯⎯ 4	9 − 4 ⎯⎯ 5	2 − 0 ⎯⎯ 2

Win with Five

2 − 2 ⎯⎯ 0	5 − 1 ⎯⎯ 4	7 − 4 ⎯⎯ 3
6 − 5 ⎯⎯ 1	4 − 1 ⎯⎯ 3	3 − 1 ⎯⎯ 2
9 − 5 ⎯⎯ 4	8 − 5 ⎯⎯ 3	7 − 2 ⎯⎯ 5

To win, be the first player to cover five game spaces.

Try Again Play again!

Play a Game

Start Put [0] [1] [2] [3] [4] [5] in a 🛍.

Get 18 red squares.
Give one game board to each player. Take turns.

Try Pick a tile. Point to an addition sentence that has that missing addend. Look for the related subtraction fact on your game board. Cover it with a square if you find it. Put the tiles back in the 🛍.

$5 + \square = 8$	$6 + \square = 9$	$3 + \square = 5$	$\square + 4 = 8$	$5 + \square = 7$
$3 + \square = 6$	$\square + 2 = 6$	$4 + \square = 9$	$8 + \square = 10$	$\square + 1 = 5$
$1 + \square = 4$	$2 + \square = 4$	$3 + \square = 10$	$\square + 5 = 5$	
$\square + 4 = 7$	$\square + 0 = 4$	$9 + \square = 10$	$\square + 5 = 10$	

Win with Five

$\begin{array}{r} 4 \\ -1 \\ \hline 3 \end{array}$	$\begin{array}{r} 7 \\ -2 \\ \hline 5 \end{array}$	$\begin{array}{r} 8 \\ -5 \\ \hline 3 \end{array}$
$\begin{array}{r} 6 \\ -3 \\ \hline 3 \end{array}$	$\begin{array}{r} 6 \\ -4 \\ \hline 2 \end{array}$	$\begin{array}{r} 5 \\ -2 \\ \hline 3 \end{array}$
$\begin{array}{r} 10 \\ -1 \\ \hline 9 \end{array}$	$\begin{array}{r} 10 \\ -3 \\ \hline 7 \end{array}$	$\begin{array}{r} 4 \\ -2 \\ \hline 2 \end{array}$

Win with Five

$\begin{array}{r} 9 \\ -5 \\ \hline 4 \end{array}$	$\begin{array}{r} 4 \\ -4 \\ \hline 0 \end{array}$	$\begin{array}{r} 5 \\ -1 \\ \hline 4 \end{array}$
$\begin{array}{r} 10 \\ -2 \\ \hline 8 \end{array}$	$\begin{array}{r} 9 \\ -6 \\ \hline 3 \end{array}$	$\begin{array}{r} 10 \\ -5 \\ \hline 5 \end{array}$
$\begin{array}{r} 5 \\ -5 \\ \hline 0 \end{array}$	$\begin{array}{r} 7 \\ -4 \\ \hline 3 \end{array}$	$\begin{array}{r} 8 \\ -4 \\ \hline 4 \end{array}$

To win, be the first player to cover five game spaces.

Try Again Play again!

Try Together

Start 🚶 Get 🎲. Get 6 red squares. Take turns.

Try Toss the 🎲. Subtract that number from 12. Say the difference. Point to a related addition fact. Cover it with a red square.

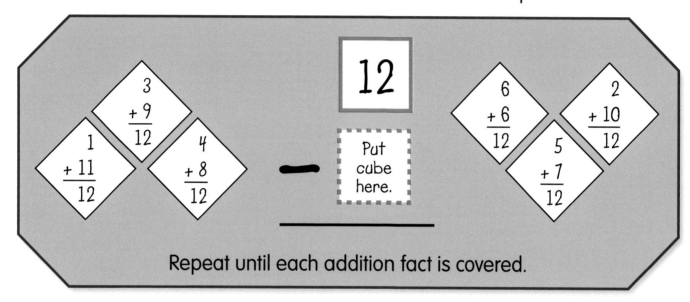

Repeat until each addition fact is covered.

Now subtract from 13!

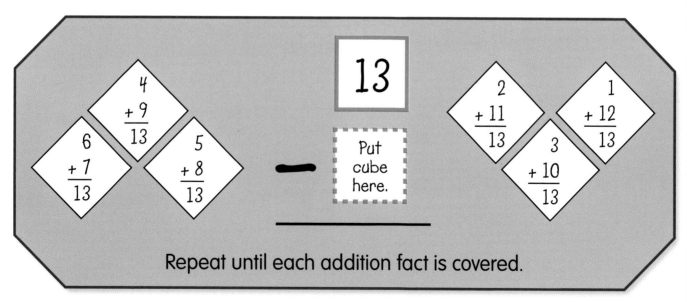

Repeat until each addition fact is covered.

Try Again Tell how you know which addition fact to use to solve a subtraction fact.

Try Together

Share your thinking while you work.

 Put [7] [8] [9] in a .

Get 12 red squares. Take turns.

Try Choose any number in a star. Pick a tile from the ⬛.
Place it below that star. Subtract those two numbers.
Say the difference. Point to a related addition fact.
Say the complete addition fact. Cover it with a red square.

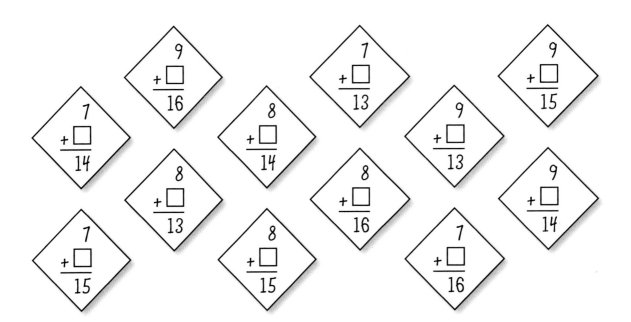

Try Again Tell how 16 minus 8 and 14 minus 7 are alike.

Center Activity 3-4 ⭐⭐

Listen and Learn

Start 👫 Put 1 2 3 4 5 6 7 8 9 in a  .

Get 12 squares. Work together.

Try Pick a tile. Say that number. Put that number of squares on the workmat.

Read Question 1. Put your tile in the first space. Say the addition sentence that helps you to find the number of missing squares.

Move your tile to the second space. Say the subtraction sentence that helps you to find the number of missing squares. Repeat these steps for Question 2.

Workmat

Question 1

If you want 11 squares in all, how many more do you need?

☐ + _____ = 11   11 − ☐ = _____

Question 2

If you want 12 squares in all, how many more do you need?

☐ + _____ = 12   12 − ☐ = _____

Try Again Repeat until the 🛍 is empty.

Listen and Learn

Partner Talk

Share your thinking while you work.

Start Get 🎲 and 🎲.
Take turns.

Try Toss 🎲 and 🎲.
Answer each question.

Put cube here. Put cube here.

How many dots are there in all?

If you want 15 dots in all, how many more dots do you need?
Point to and say the number sentence that helps you to find the number of missing dots.

$15 - 2 = $ _____
$15 - 3 = $ _____
$15 - 4 = $ _____
$15 - 5 = $ _____
$15 - 6 = $ _____
$15 - 7 = $ _____
$15 - 8 = $ _____
$15 - 9 = $ _____
$15 - 10 = $ _____
$15 - 11 = $ _____
$15 - 12 = $ _____

If you want 16 dots in all, how many more dots do you need?
Point to and say the number sentence that helps you to find the number of missing dots.

$16 - 2 = $ _____
$16 - 3 = $ _____
$16 - 4 = $ _____
$16 - 5 = $ _____
$16 - 6 = $ _____
$16 - 7 = $ _____
$16 - 8 = $ _____
$16 - 9 = $ _____
$16 - 10 = $ _____
$16 - 11 = $ _____
$16 - 12 = $ _____

Try Again Repeat until each player gets 5 or more turns.
Talk about why knowing how to add helps you to subtract.

Look and See

Partner Talk

Share your thinking while you work.

Start  Get 8 9 . Get 18 red squares.

Look at each chart. Talk about what each number tells you. Take turns.

Try Read a question. Use squares to help you find the answer. Put a tile in the chart to show the answer.

1. How many apples were not sold?
2. How many bags of popcorn were sold?
3. How many cups of lemonade were not sold?

Snacks at the Carnival

	sold	not sold	total
apple	9	?	16
popcorn	?	8	17
lemonade	7	?	13

Storybook Favorites

	read	not read	total
The Three Little Pigs	?	10	15
The Three Bears	9	?	13
Snow White	?	6	14

1. How many children read <u>Snow White</u>?
2. How many children did not read <u>The Three Bears</u>?
3. How many children read <u>The Three Little Pigs</u>?

Try Again Pick a chart. For each row, say the subtraction sentence that helps you to find the answer.

Look and See

Start ✳ Get

and 1 2 3 4 5 6 7 8 9 .

Get 18 red squares. Look at each chart.
Talk about what each number tells you. Take turns.

Try Read a question. Explain how to find the answer using squares. Then say a number sentence. Put a tile in the chart to show the answer.

1. How many children do not have a ball?
2. How many children have a jump rope?
3. How many children do not have a toy car?

Toys

	have	do not have	total
Beach Ball	7	?	11
Jump Rope	?	9	16
Car	8	?	17

Favorite Juices

	like	do not like	total
Apple			12
Grape			10
Orange			14

Use number tiles. Show one number in each row in the Favorite Juices chart. Ask your partner questions so that your partner can find the missing number in each row.

Try Again Remove the tiles. Find different ways to complete the Favorite Juices chart.

Helping Hands

Start 🧑‍🤝‍🧑 Get 10 red squares. Take turns.

Try Hold up some fingers. Say that number.
Have your partner point to that number of jars.
How many beans are in those jars in all?
Ask your partner to count them by tens.
Use a square to cover each jar your partner counts.

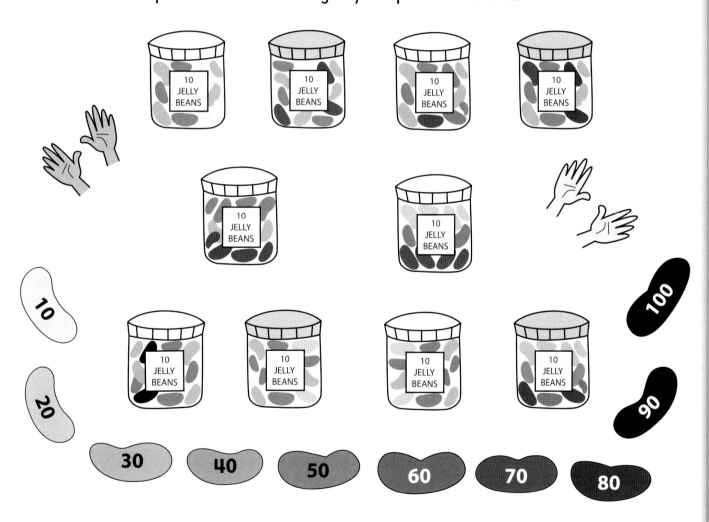

Count back by tens together as you remove the squares.

Try Again Repeat until each player gets 5 turns.

Helping Hands

Share your thinking while you work.

Start 👥 Get 10 red squares. Take turns.

Try Hold up some fingers. Say that number. Have your partner point to that number of bags. How many marbles are in those bags? Ask your partner to count them by tens. Put a square on each bag your partner counts. Point to the place value blocks and the number name for the marbles in those bags.
Repeat until each player gets 5 turns.

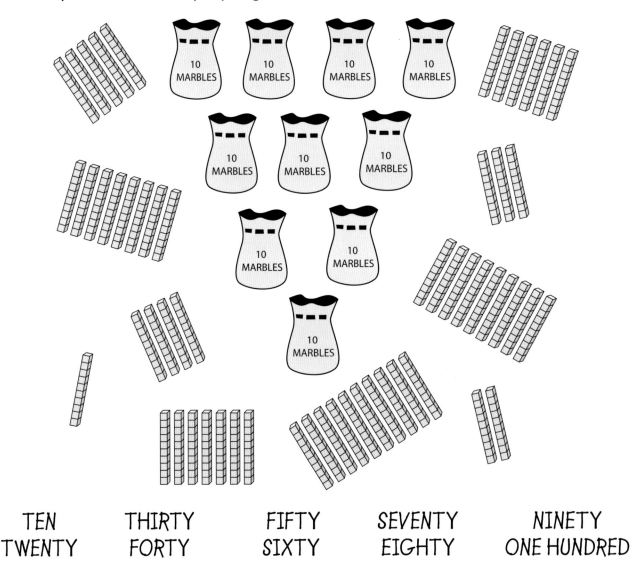

| TEN | THIRTY | FIFTY | SEVENTY | NINETY |
| TWENTY | FORTY | SIXTY | EIGHTY | ONE HUNDRED |

Try Again Try to spell the number names without looking.

Math in Motion

Partner Talk
Share your thinking while you work.

Start 👫 Put 1 2 3 4 5 6 7 8 9 in a 🛍.

Take turns.

Try Pick two tiles. Put them on the workmat to make a number that has tens and ones. Say that number together. Look at the tens place. Flash ten fingers for each ten you count. Ask your partner to look at the ones place and flash one finger for each one.

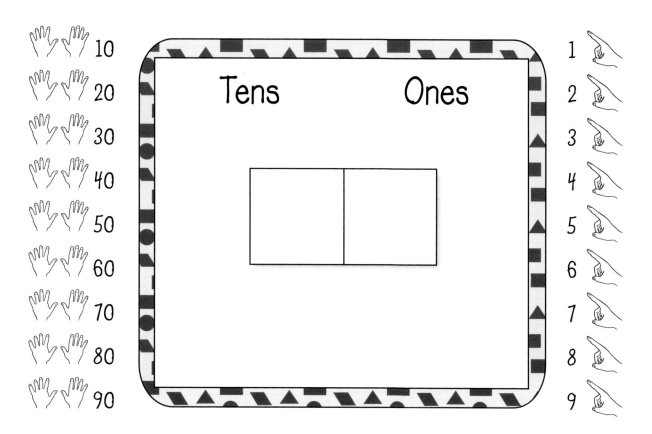

10		1
20		2
30	**Tens** **Ones**	3
40		4
50		5
60		6
70		7
80		8
90		9

Put the tiles back in the 🛍.
Repeat until each player gets 5 turns.

Try Again Talk about how numbers that have tens and ones are like dimes and pennies.

Math in Motion

Partner Talk

Share your thinking while you work.

Start 👥 Get ⌈1⌉ ⌈2⌉ ⌈3⌉ ⌈4⌉ ⌈5⌉ ⌈6⌉ ⌈7⌉ ⌈8⌉ ⌈9⌉.

Take turns.

Try Choose and say any two-digit number that has a different number of tens and ones. Find the tile for the tens place in your number. Put it on the workmat. Have your partner find the tile for the ones place in your number. Put it on the workmat. Say that number together. Flash ten fingers for each ten in that number.
Have your partner flash one finger for each one in that number.

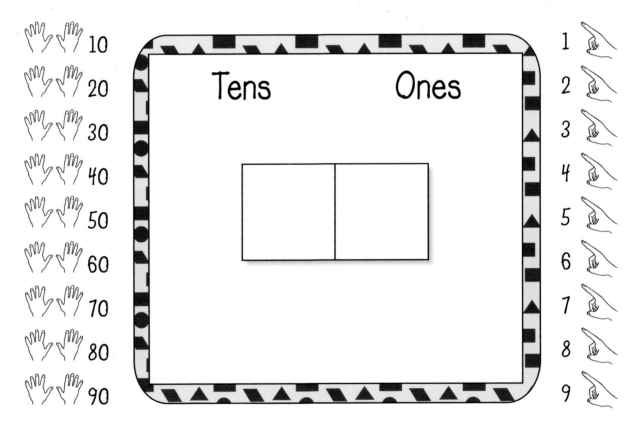

Change the order of the tiles. Flash fingers for that number.
Repeat until each player gets 5 turns.

Try Again Look around the classroom. Find a two-digit number.
Flash fingers for that number.

Look and See

Start  Get ⓪ ① ② ③ ④ ⑤ ⑥ ⑦ ⑧ ⑨ .

Take turns.

Try Point to a word name. Ask your partner to show that number with tiles and say that number. Change the order of the tiles. Say the word name for the new number. If that word name is on the page, shake hands.

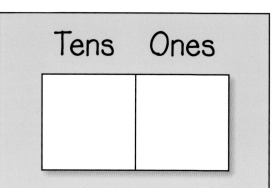

Tens   Ones

Twenty-one

Ninety-six

Fifty-nine

Twenty-four

Thirty-four

Thirty-two

Sixty-nine

Seventeen

Forty-two

Sixty-five

Seventy-one

Fifty-six

Eighty-six

Twelve

Ninety-five

Repeat until you use all of the word names.

Try Again Talk about how seventeen and seventy-one are different.

Look and See

Partner Talk
Share your thinking while you work.

Start 👫 Get  0 1 2 3 4 5 6 7 8 9 .

Work together.

Try Pick three tiles. Make a two-digit number. Point to one or two words to name your number. See how many other two-digit numbers you can make and name with those three tiles. Repeat the activity 5 times.

Twenty
Thirty
Forty
Fifty
Sixty
Seventy
Eighty
Ninety

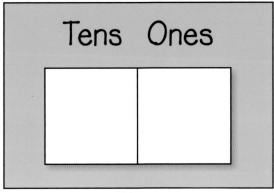

Tens   Ones

Ten
Eleven
Twelve
Thirteen
Fourteen
Fifteen
Sixteen
Seventeen
Eighteen
Nineteen

One
Two
Three
Four
Five
Six
Seven
Eight
Nine

Try Again Point to a word name.
Ask your partner to show that number with tiles.

Center Activity 4-3 ⭐ ⭐

Cover Three

Partner Talk

Share your thinking while you work.

Start 🚶 Put 1 2 3 4 5 6 7 8 9 in a 🛍️.

Get 6 red squares. Get 6 blue squares. Take turns.

Try Pick two tiles. Make a two-digit number. Say that number. Do you see a number greater than your number on the game board?

  If **YES**, put a square on it.

  If **NO**, lose your turn.

Put the tiles back in the 🛍️. Take turns until one player wins.

42	18	36
39	57	91
64	48	72

To win, get: ■ ■ ■ or ■ or ■ or ■
                          ■   ■   ■
                          ■   ■   ■

Try Again Play again! This time, find a number that is less than your number.

Cover Three

Start  Put  in a 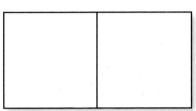 .

Get 6 red squares. Get 6 blue squares. Take turns.

Try Pick two tiles. Make a two-digit number. Say that number. Look at the game board. Can you find a sentence that matches your number?

> If **YES**, say that sentence and put a square on it.

> If **NO**, lose your turn. Put the tiles back in the .

Take turns until one player wins.

My number is less than 50.	My number is greater than 11.	My number is less than 39.
My number is greater than 45.	My number is less than 70.	My number is greater than 27.
My number is less than 80.	My number is greater than 62.	My number is less than 98.

To win, get: ■ ■ ■ or or

Try Again Remove your squares. Play again.

Center Activity 4-4 ★ ★

Look and See

Start 👫 Get 1 1 2 2 3 3 4 4 5 5 6 6 7 7 8 8 9 9 . Work together.

Try

99	25	72	85	94	52	97	41
56	23	19	64	34	38	18	29

Use two tiles. Show a number from the rectangle here.

Use two tiles. Show another number from the rectangle here.

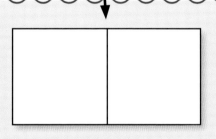

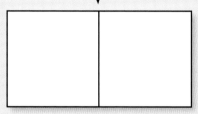

Make sure the number on the left is greater.

Say: "____ is greater than ____."

Now put the two numbers in a different order below.

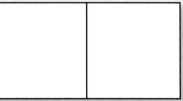

Make sure the number on the left is less.

Say: "____ is less than ____."

Try Again Remove the tiles. Repeat the activity.
Choose other numbers from the rectangle.

Look and See

Start Get

Take turns.

Try Place twelve number tiles on the page so that you can say each sentence.

Say: "___ is greater than ___."

Say: "___ is less than ___."

Say: "___ is equal to ___."

Try Again Remove the tiles. Choose different tiles. Repeat the activity.

Partner Talk

Share your thinking while you work.

Start  Get 18 red squares. Get 9 blue squares.
Cover the stars with the blue squares.
Give one game board to each player. Take turns.

Try Uncover one star. Say the number. Look on the game boards.
Which number comes after that number? Any player who has
the answer can cover it with a red square. Set aside the blue square.
Repeat until one player wins.

| 13 | 56 | 61 | 33 |

| 95 | 87 | 42 | 27 | 70 |

1	2	3	4	5	6	7	8	9	10
11	12	13	14	15	16	17	18	19	20
21	22	23	24	25	26	27	28	29	30
31	32	33	34	35	36	37	38	39	40
41	42	43	44	45	46	47	48	49	50
51	52	53	54	55	56	57	58	59	60
61	62	63	64	65	66	67	68	69	70
71	72	73	74	75	76	77	78	79	80
81	82	83	84	85	86	87	88	89	90
91	92	93	94	95	96	97	98	99	100

Four Corners

96	57	34
88	14	28
43	62	71

Four Corners

88	28	14
43	34	96
57	71	62

To win, be the first player to cover four corners.

Try Again Play again!

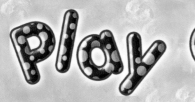 

Partner Talk
Share your thinking while you work.

Start 👥 Get 18 red squares. Get 9 blue squares.
Cover the stars with the blue squares.
Give one game board to each player. Take turns.

Try Uncover one star. Say the number. Look on the game boards.
Which number comes before or after that number? Any player who
has one of those answers can cover it with a red square. Set aside the
blue square. Repeat until one player wins.

1	2	3	4	5	6	7	8	9	10
11	12	13	14	15	16	17	18	19	20
21	22	23	24	25	26	27	28	29	30
31	32	33	34	35	36	37	38	39	40
41	42	43	44	45	46	47	48	49	50
51	52	53	54	55	56	57	58	59	60
61	62	63	64	65	66	67	68	69	70
71	72	73	74	75	76	77	78	79	80
81	82	83	84	85	86	87	88	89	90
91	92	93	94	95	96	97	98	99	100

Stars: 65, 89, 48, 96, 51, 30, 18, 12, 22

Four Corners

64	73	90
19	58	95
47	23	29

Four Corners

56	21	88
49	66	31
17	97	71

To win, be the first player to cover four corners.

Try Again Play again!

Center Activity 4-6

Helping Hands

Partner Talk

Share your thinking while you work.

 Get 🎲. Get ⟦0⟧⟦1⟧⟦2⟧⟦3⟧⟦4⟧⟦5⟧⟦6⟧⟦7⟧⟦8⟧⟦9⟧

and ⟦0⟧⟦1⟧⟦2⟧⟦3⟧⟦4⟧⟦5⟧⟦6⟧⟦7⟧⟦8⟧⟦9⟧ . Take turns.

 Toss the 🎲.

Follow directions for ordering three numbers.

Use number tiles to show these numbers in order.

⚀	41, 10, 32	⚁	11, 99, 77
⚁	88, 21, 71	⚄	63, 36, 28
⚂	54, 63, 45	⚅	43, 85, 24

Put your numbers in order from least to greatest with help from your partner.

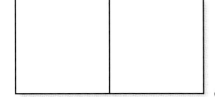   ,   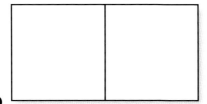   ,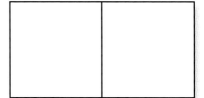

Least   **Between**   **Greatest**

Use the hundred chart to explain why the numbers are in order.

1	2	3	4	5	6	7	8	9	10
11	12	13	14	15	16	17	18	19	20
21	22	23	24	25	26	27	28	29	30
31	32	33	34	35	36	37	38	39	40
41	42	43	44	45	46	47	48	49	50
51	52	53	54	55	56	57	58	59	60
61	62	63	64	65	66	67	68	69	70
71	72	73	74	75	76	77	78	79	80
81	82	83	84	85	86	87	88	89	90
91	92	93	94	95	96	97	98	99	100

Try Again Talk about how numbers are ordered on a calendar.

Helping Hands

Start 👥 Get ⓪ ① ② ③ ④ ⑤ ⑥ ⑦ ⑧ ⑨ and

⓪ ① ② ③ ④ ⑤ ⑥ ⑦ ⑧ ⑨ . Work Together.

Show tiles for any two-digit number here.

Ask your partner to show any two-digit number here.

Show a number that you choose together from a circle.

1	2	3	4	5	6	7	8	9	10
11	12	13	14	15	16	17	18	19	20
21	22	23	24	25	26	27	28	29	30
31	32	33	34	35	36	37	38	39	40
41	42	43	44	45	46	47	48	49	50
51	52	53	54	55	56	57	58	59	60
61	62	63	64	65	66	67	68	69	70
71	72	73	74	75	76	77	78	79	80
81	82	83	84	85	86	87	88	89	90
91	92	93	94	95	96	97	98	99	100

82   16   51

39   63   24

Order your numbers from least to greatest.

Least , Between , Greatest

Now order your numbers from greatest to least.

Greatest , Between , Least

Try Again Talk about how you know which number is greatest.

Listen and Learn

Partner Talk
Share your thinking while you work.

Start 🏃 Get 6 red squares. Take turns.

Try Pick a rectangle. Read the directions.
Follow directions by moving a finger on the hundred chart.
Cover the directions with a square when you finish.

Begin at 5. Count by fives. Take turns with your partner.	Begin at 50. Count back by fives by yourself. Clap with each number.	Begin at 100. Count back by tens with your partner. Pat your knees, then clap your hands.
Begin at 2. Count by twos by yourself.	Begin at 10. Count by tens. Stomp with each number. Take turns.	Begin at 50. Count back by twos by yourself. Clap or snap your fingers.

1	2	3	4	5	6	7	8	9	10
11	12	13	14	15	16	17	18	19	20
21	22	23	24	25	26	27	28	29	30
31	32	33	34	35	36	37	38	39	40
41	42	43	44	45	46	47	48	49	50
51	52	53	54	55	56	57	58	59	60
61	62	63	64	65	66	67	68	69	70
71	72	73	74	75	76	77	78	79	80
81	82	83	84	85	86	87	88	89	90
91	92	93	94	95	96	97	98	99	100

Try Again Uncover the directions. Try again. Choose directions you did not follow the first time.

Listen and Learn

Start 👫 Get 5 red squares. Take turns.

Try Pick an activity from a rectangle. Read the directions. Follow directions. Use the hundred chart if you need it. Cover the directions with a square when you finish.

> Begin at 100.
> Count back by fives.
> Tap your foot as you
> say each number.

> Begin at 11. Count all
> the numbers that have
> the same digits. Clap
> twice on each number.

> Begin at 13.
> Count by twos.
> Take turns as you
> clap each number.

> Begin at 83.
> Count back by tens
> alone. Blink your eyes
> as you count.

> Begin at 4.
> Count by tens with
> your partner.
> Clap each other's hands.

1	2	3	4	5	6	7	8	9	10
11	12	13	14	15	16	17	18	19	20
21	22	23	24	25	26	27	28	29	30
31	32	33	34	35	36	37	38	39	40
41	42	43	44	45	46	47	48	49	50
51	52	53	54	55	56	57	58	59	60
61	62	63	64	65	66	67	68	69	70
71	72	73	74	75	76	77	78	79	80
81	82	83	84	85	86	87	88	89	90
91	92	93	94	95	96	97	98	99	100

Try Again Uncover the directions. Try again.
See if you can make another pattern as you count.

Look and See

Start 👫 Get 6 red squares. Get 6 blue squares.
Take turns.

Try Take a trip through the garden. Find an anthill.
Count the ants around it. If there is an even number
of ants, put a red square on the anthill. If there is an
odd number of ants, put a blue square on the anthill.

Try Again Begin again! This time, tell if the number of ants will be even or
odd if one more ant joins the group. Or, count the number of
students in your class and tell if the number is even or odd.

Look and See

Partner Talk
Share your thinking while you work.

Start 👬 Get 🎲 🎲 🎲. Get 18 red squares.
Get 1 blue square. Take turns.

Try Toss 🎲 🎲 🎲. Add the numbers and say the sum. Use red squares on the workmat to show if the number is even or odd.

Your partner finds your number near a frog and puts the blue square on it. Together, skip count by 2 from that number up to 17 or 18. Play until each partner gets 5 or more turns.

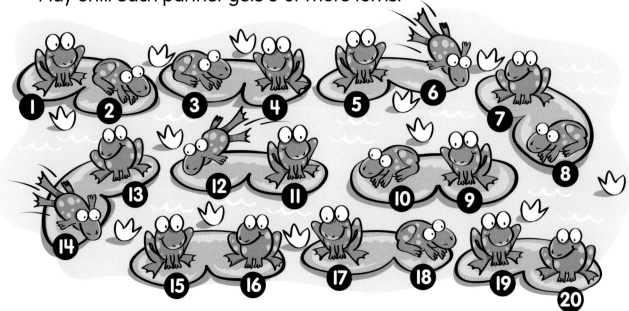

Try Again Begin again! This time, skip count backwards by 2 from your number back to 1 or 2.

Try Together

Partner Talk

Share your thinking while you work.

Start 🚶 Get 10 red squares.

Try Read the chart with your partner. Talk about the number of cups sold on Monday, Tuesday, Wednesday, and Friday. Then read the question and the clues below the chart. Use red squares to cover the numbers that do not match the clues.

Some children set up a lemonade stand.
They kept track of the number of cups they sold.

Cups of Lemonade Sold Each 🥤 = 10 cups	
Monday	🥤 🥤 🥤 🥤
Tuesday	🥤
Wednesday	🥤 🥤 🥤
Thursday	?
Friday	🥤 🥤 🥤 🥤 🥤

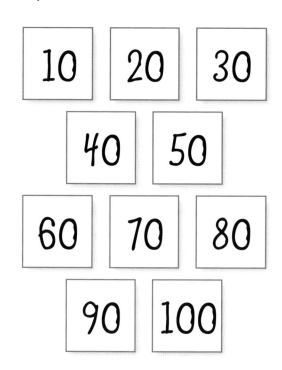

How many cups were sold on Thursday?

CLUES
1. They sold less than 90 cups.
2. They sold more than 50 cups.
3. The digit in the tens place is an odd number.

Try Again How many more cups were sold on Friday than on Tuesday? Make up other questions. Answer each other's questions.

Try Together

Partner Talk

Share your thinking while you work.

Start 👤 Get 10 red squares.

Try DO THIS FOR EACH CHART. Read the chart with your partner. Talk about what the pictures tell you. Then read the question and the clues below the chart. Use red squares to cover the numbers at the bottom of the page that do not match the clues. Answer the question.

Fruits in the Fruit Bowl Each picture means 5 fruits	
Apples	🍎🍎🍎
Bananas	🍌🍌🍌🍌🍌
Cherries	?
Pears	🍐🍐🍐🍐🍐🍐
Oranges	🍊🍊🍊🍊🍊

Buttons in the Jar Each ⊛ = 5 buttons	
Red	⊛⊛⊛⊛⊛⊛
Blue	⊛⊛
Yellow	⊛⊛⊛⊛⊛
Green	⊛
Pink	?

How many cherries are in the fruit bowl?

CLUES

1. There are more cherries than pears.
2. There are fewer than 50 cherries.
3. The number of cherries is an even number.

How many pink buttons are in the jar?

CLUES

1. There are more pink than blue buttons.
2. There are fewer pink than yellow buttons.
3. The number of pink buttons is an odd number.

5	10	15	20	25
30	35	40	45	50

Try Again Tell how many more red buttons there are than yellow buttons. Make up other questions. Answer each other's questions.

Center Activity 4-10

Try Together

Partner Talk

Share your thinking while you work.

Start Get   . Get 10 squares. Take turns.

Try Choose any three coins.
Put a under each coin you choose.
Ask your partner to count your money.
Use a square to cover that amount of money.

| 21¢ | 30¢ | 16¢ | 11¢ | 3¢ |
| 12¢ | 15¢ | 25¢ | 20¢ | 7¢ |

Try Again Repeat until every amount of money is covered.

Try Together

Start 👫 Get   . Get 15 squares.
Cover each amount of money with a square. Take turns.

Try Uncover an amount of money. Use exactly four coins to get
that amount. Put a under each coin you choose.
Ask your partner to count your money.

40¢	13¢	20¢	31¢	8¢
21¢	35¢	26¢	16¢	4¢
25¢	17¢	22¢	12¢	30¢

Try Again Repeat until every amount of money is uncovered.

Look and See

Start 🚶 Get ⫘ ⫘ ⫘ ⫘ ⫘ ⫘ ⫘ .

Take turns.

Try Choose a piggy bank. Place a ⫘ under each coin in that bank. Work with your partner to count that amount of money.

1 quarter
2 dimes

1 half-dollar
1 quarter
1 penny

1 quarter
6 pennies

1 half-dollar
3 nickels

1 half-dollar
2 dimes

2 quarters
2 dimes
1 nickel

Repeat until you use every bank.

Try Again Point to a bank that has each amount of money:
70¢, 31¢, 75¢, 45¢, 65¢, 76¢.

Look and See

Partner Talk
Share your thinking while you work.

Start 👥 Get 18 red squares. Take turns.

Try Choose a piggy bank. Choose coins to make that amount of money.
Put a square next to each coin you choose.
Have your partner make the same amount using different coins.

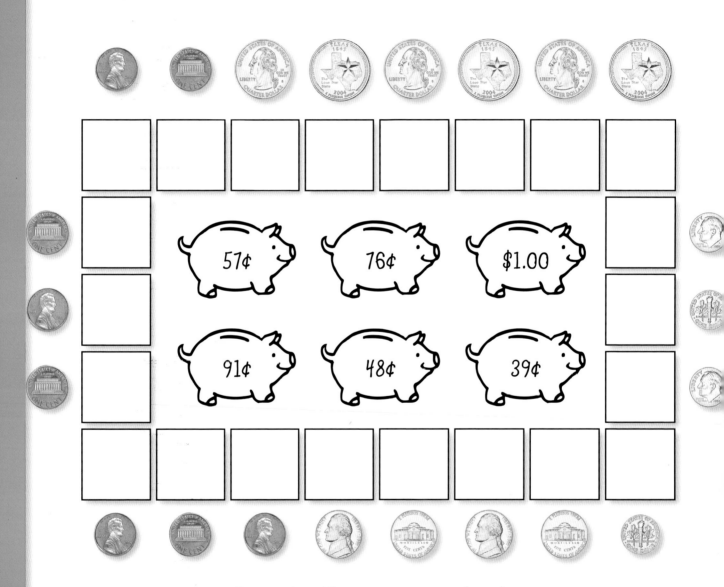

57¢ 76¢ $1.00

91¢ 48¢ 39¢

Repeat until you use every bank.

Try Again Talk about when you have used half-dollars or quarters.

Center Activity 5-2 ⭐ ⭐

Play a Game

Partner Talk

Share your thinking while you work.

Start 👫 Get 18 red squares. Get 9 blue squares.
Cover the jars with blue squares.
Give one game board to each player. Take turns.

Try Remove one blue square. Count that amount of money.
Look for that amount on the game boards.
Any player who has the answer covers it with a red square.

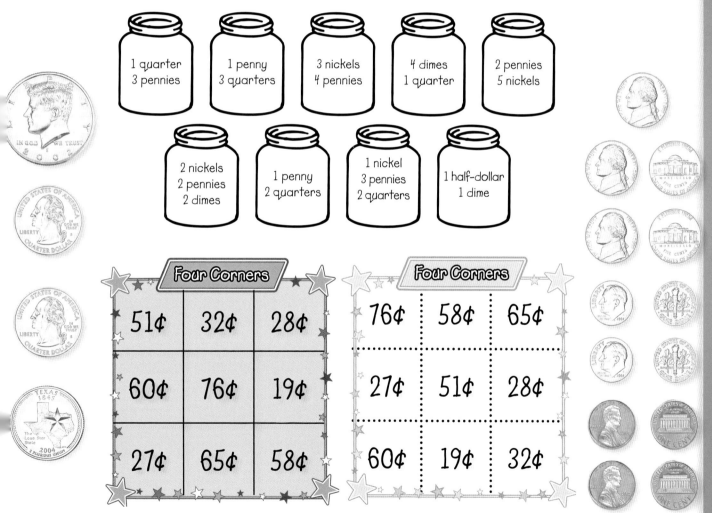

| 1 quarter 3 pennies | 1 penny 3 quarters | 3 nickels 4 pennies | 4 dimes 1 quarter | 2 pennies 5 nickels |

| 2 nickels 2 pennies 2 dimes | 1 penny 2 quarters | 1 nickel 3 pennies 2 quarters | 1 half-dollar 1 dime |

Four Corners

51¢	32¢	28¢
60¢	76¢	19¢
27¢	65¢	58¢

Four Corners

76¢	58¢	65¢
27¢	51¢	28¢
60¢	19¢	32¢

To win, be the first player who covers four corners.

Try Again Play again!

 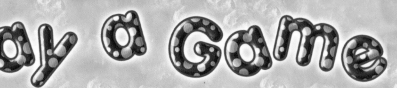 

Partner Talk
Share your thinking while you work.

 **Start** 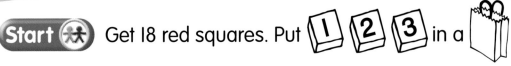 Get 18 red squares. Put [1] [2] [3] in a 🛍.

Give one game board to each player. Take turns.

Try Point to a jar. Tell how much money is in the jar.
Take a tile from the 🛍. Add 1¢, or 2¢, or 3¢.
How much money is that in all? Look on the game board.
Any player who has the answer covers it with a red square.
Put the tile back in the 🛍.

3 quarters
1 penny

1 half-dollar
1 nickel

1 quarter
2 dimes

3 dimes
3 nickels

2 quarters
5 pennies

2 quarters
2 dimes
1 nickel
1 penny

Four Corners

77¢	57¢	56¢
48¢	47¢	58¢
79¢	78¢	46¢

Four Corners

58¢	47¢	78¢
79¢	56¢	77¢
48¢	57¢	46¢

To win, be the first player who covers four corners.

Try Again Play again!

Helping Hands

Partner Talk
Share your thinking while you work.

Start 🏃 Get 14 red squares. Take turns.

Try Point to a circle. Say that amount of money. Ask your partner to point to another circle so that the total amount of money is $1.00. If you are sure that you have $1.00, cover each amount of money with a square. Repeat until you use every circle.

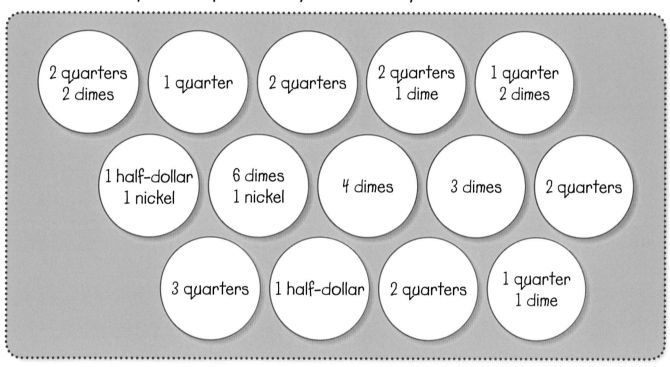

2 quarters 2 dimes

1 quarter

2 quarters

2 quarters 1 dime

1 quarter 2 dimes

1 half-dollar 1 nickel

6 dimes 1 nickel

4 dimes

3 dimes

2 quarters

3 quarters

1 half-dollar

2 quarters

1 quarter 1 dime

Try Again Repeat the activity.

Helping Hands

Share your thinking while you work.

Start Get ⬭ ⬭ ⬭ ⬭.

Get 9 red squares. Cover the stars with those squares.
Take turns.

Try Uncover a star. Say that amount of money.
How much more money do you need to make $1.00?
Put ⬭ under 1, 2, 3, or 4 coins to show the
extra money you need to make $1.00.

95¢   25¢   90¢   50¢

75¢   65¢   40¢   85¢   35¢

Try Again Repeat the activity. This time, try to use different coins
to make one dollar.

Listen and Learn

Partner Talk

Share your thinking while you work.

Start 👫 Get one 🎲. Take turns.

Try Toss the 🎲. Follow the directions. Use the money next to your toss.

Toss	Count the money. Make sure your partner hears you. Ask your partner to point to the total below.
⚀	[2 one-dollar bills, dime, nickel, 3 pennies]
⚁	[2 one-dollar bills, quarter, quarter, dime, nickel, penny]
⚂	[1 one-dollar bill, quarter, quarter, dime, dime, dime, dime, nickel]
⚃	[1 one-dollar bill, quarter, dime, dime, dime, penny, penny, penny]
⚄	[1 one-dollar bill, quarter, quarter, dime, dime, nickel, penny, penny, penny]
⚅	[1 one-dollar bill, quarter, quarter, quarter, dime, dime, penny, penny]

$2.91 $1.97 $1.86
$2.18 $1.78 $1.58

Try Again Point to an amount of money. Read the amount in dollars and cents. Ask your partner to count bills and coins for that amount of money.

Center Activity 5-5 ★

Listen and Learn

Start 👤 Get one . Get 14 red squares. Take turns.

Try Put a below an amount of money.
Read the dollars and cents. Show that amount of money below.
Place a red square next to each bill and coin that you use.

$1.56

$1.65

$2.38

$2.83

$1.12

$1.21

$1.75

$1.57

Try Again Put red squares next to some bills and coins.
Ask your partner to count and say the total amount of money.

Center Activity 5-5 ⭐ ⭐

Look and See

Partner Talk

Share your thinking while you work.

Start Get 0 1 2 3 4 5 6 7 .Take turns.

Try Complete both lists. Use each tile exactly once.

Find a way to make
45¢ in each row.

	4	1
0	2	
0	3	
	2	0

Find a way to make
65¢ in each row.

1		0
	1	1
0		1
0	3	

Try Again Can you find one more way to make 45¢ or 65¢?

Look and See

Start 👤 Get ⬜0 ⬜1 ⬜2 ⬜3 ⬜4 ⬜5 ⬜6 ⬜7 ⬜8 ⬜9 .

Take turns.

Try Complete both lists. Use each tile exactly once.

Find a way to make $1.00 in each row.

Quarter	Dime	Nickel
	0	0
2	1	
	5	
1		1

Find a way to make 85¢ in each row.

Quarter	Dime	Nickel
0	4	
2	1	
1	3	
2	2	
2	3	

Try Again Find other ways to make 85¢ or $1.00.

Start 👥 Get a 🎲.
Get I red square for one player.
Get I blue square for the other player. Take turns.

Try Toss the 🎲. Move that many spaces on the game board.
When you land on a space, read and follow the directions.
Say the sum. The first player to reach the beach
on an exact toss wins.

15 add 2 tens	3 add 4 tens	25 add 3 tens	36 add 5 tens	17 add 1 ten	11 add 3 tens	41 add 4 tens	86 add 1 ten
							67 add 3 tens
						32 add 5 tens	8 add 2 tens
					19 add 2 tens	61 add 1 ten	
					51 add 1 ten		
Welcome to Rainbow Beach	46 add 3 tens	72 add 2 tens	30 add 5 tens	49 add 4 tens	12 add 2 tens		

Try Again Tell why it can be helpful to use mental math to add tens.

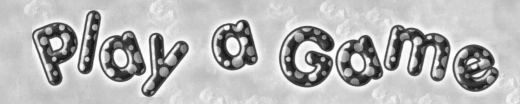

Share your thinking while you work.

Start 👥 Get a 🎲.
Get I red square for one player.
Get I blue square for the other player. Take turns.

Try Toss the 🎲. Move forward that many spaces on the game board. When you land on a space, look at the first number. Tell how many tens you would add to get to the second number. The first player to reach the beach on an exact toss wins.

Start	35 to 55	17 to 47	11 to 21	65 to 75	42 to 82	57 to 77	16 to 46	30 to 80
								85 to 95
							73 to 93	22 to 52
						50 to 90	1 to 71	
						32 to 72		
Welcome to Rainbow Beach	10 to 80	43 to 63	27 to 97	13 to 33	54 to 64			

Try Again Tell what happens to the tens place of a two-digit number when tens are added to it.

Try Together

Start 👥 Put  4 5 6 7 8 9 in a 🛍.

Get 19 red squares.
Get 9 blue squares.

Try Pick a number in a balloon. Put that number of red squares in the two ten-frames on the left. Your partner picks a tile from the 🛍 and uses blue squares to show that number in the ten-frame on the right. Add the number of red squares and the number of blue squares. Can you make a ten? Say the sum together.

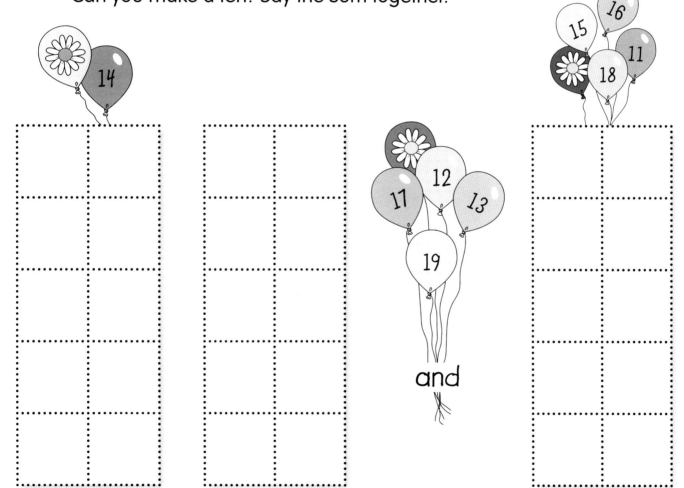

Try Again For each number, tell how many more ones you need to make the next ten.

Try Together

Partner Talk

Share your thinking while you work.

Start 👥 Put 4 5 6 7 8 9 in a 🛍️ .

Get 18 red squares.
Get 9 blue squares.

Try Pick a number on a balloon. Show it in the ten–frames on the left using red squares. Your partner picks a tile from the 🛍️ and tries to say the sum using mental math. Check by adding that number of blue squares. If your partner's mental math is correct, shake hands.

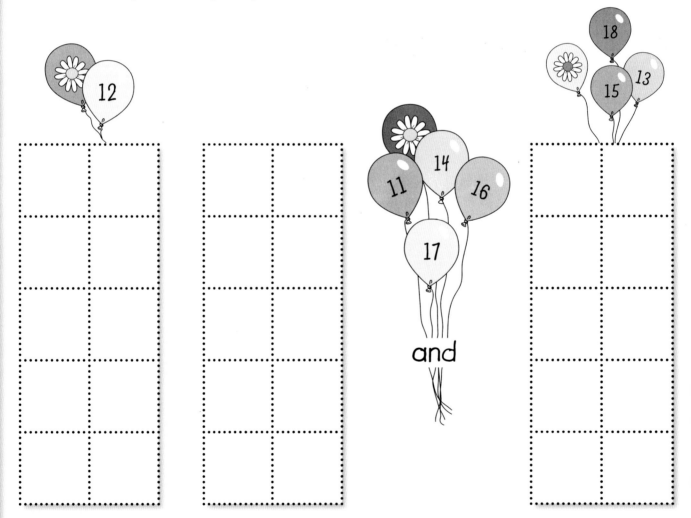

12

14

11

16

17

and

18

15

13

Try Again How do you know if the number of squares in all is more than 20, less than 20, or 20?

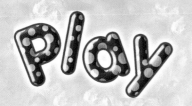  

Start 👥 Get 12 red squares.

Cover each game space with a square. Take turns.

Try Uncover two game spaces.

If you uncover an addition problem and the sum for that problem, keep the squares.

If not, put the squares back where they were.

Take turns until all the spaces are uncovered.

Memory Match

52 + 17	86	25 + 13	13 + 43
87	41 + 27	69	54 + 32
56	68	52 + 35	38

To win, collect the most squares.

Try Again Play again!

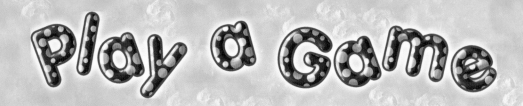

Start 👫 Get 12 red squares.

Cover each game space with a square. Take turns.

Try Uncover two game spaces.

If you uncover two addition problems that have the same sum, explain why. Keep the squares.

If not, put the squares back where they were.

Take turns until all the spaces are uncovered.

Memory Match

25 + 24	34 + 53	11 + 68	17 + 32
81 + 18	12 + 66	31 + 47	13 + 56
22 + 47	42 + 37	25 + 62	51 + 48

To win, collect the most squares.

Try Again Play again!

Helping Hands

Partner Talk
Share your thinking while you work.

Start 👫 Take turns until each of you gets 5 or more turns.

Try Choose an umbrella and point to that number on the hundred chart.
Have your partner point to a number on a duck.
Add it to your number. Move down to add the tens, and
move to the right to add the ones.

Try Again This time, start with a number on a duck.
Then add a number on an umbrella.

Center Activity 6-4 ⭐   Topic 6   **7**

Helping Hands

Partner Talk

Share your thinking while you work.

Start 👫 Put [1] [2] [3] [4] [5] in a 🛍.

Take turns until each of you gets 5 or more turns.

Try Pick a number on a skateboard. Point to it on the hundred chart. Let your partner pick two tiles and make a two-digit number.

Add that number to yours by moving down to add the tens, and over to the right to add the ones. Say the sum. Put the tiles back in the 🛍.

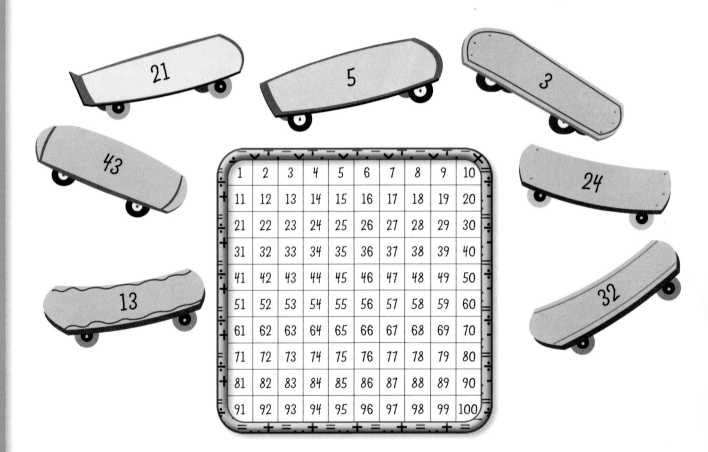

1	2	3	4	5	6	7	8	9	10
11	12	13	14	15	16	17	18	19	20
21	22	23	24	25	26	27	28	29	30
31	32	33	34	35	36	37	38	39	40
41	42	43	44	45	46	47	48	49	50
51	52	53	54	55	56	57	58	59	60
61	62	63	64	65	66	67	68	69	70
71	72	73	74	75	76	77	78	79	80
81	82	83	84	85	86	87	88	89	90
91	92	93	94	95	96	97	98	99	100

21 5 3 43 24 13 32

Try Again This time, try using your own numbers.

Look and See

Start 🚹 Work together.

Try Choose **a**, **b**, **c**, or **d**.
Say the number of blocks in each tower.
Explain the pattern. How many blocks will it take to build the fifth tower? How many blocks will it take to build the sixth tower?

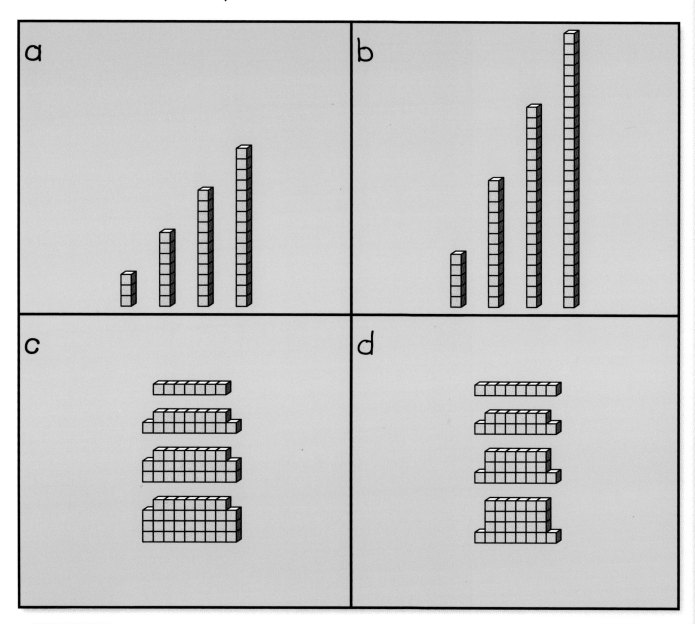

Try Again Choose **a**, **b**, **c**, or **d**. How many blocks does it take to build the first three towers?

Look and See

Partner Talk

Share your thinking while you work.

Start 👥 Work together.

Try Choose a chart. Explain the pattern. Find the towers with that pattern. How many blocks will it take to build the sixth tower?

Tower	Blocks
1	8
2	13
3	18
4	23
5	28

Tower	Blocks
1	6
2	16
3	26
4	36
5	46

Tower	Blocks
1	9
2	15
3	21
4	27
5	33

Tower	Blocks
1	7
2	14
3	21
4	28
5	35

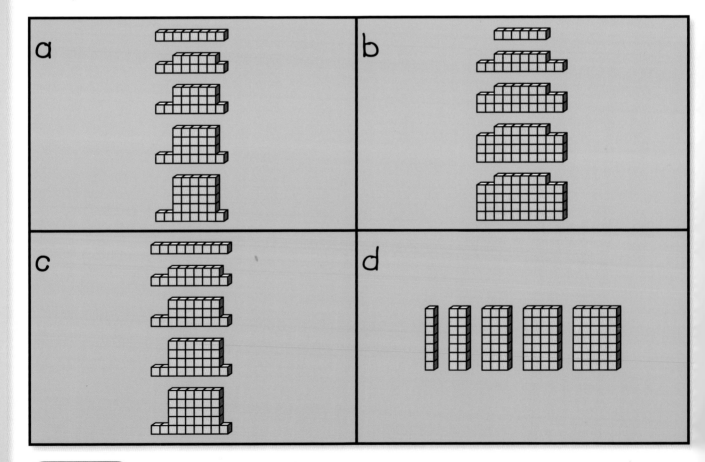

Try Again Choose **a**, **b**, **c**, or **d**. How many blocks does it take to build the first three towers?

Cover Three

Start  Get a . Get 6 red squares. Get 6 blue squares. Take turns.

Try Pick a number in a circle. Toss the .
Subtract that many tens. Say the difference.

If you see the difference on the game board,
cover it with a square.

If not lose your turn.

 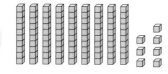   

57	87	63
37	13	77
43	47	53

To win, get: ■■■ or ■ or ■   or ■
                     ■   ■   ■   ■
                     ■   ■   ■

Try Again Talk about how you subtract tens.
Use the place-value blocks to explain what you do.

Center Activity 7-1 ⭐

Cover Three

Partner
Talk

Share your thinking while you work.

Start  Put ⌐1⌐ ⌐2⌐ ⌐3⌐ ⌐4⌐ ⌐5⌐ ⌐6⌐ in a 🛍.

Get 6 red squares. Get 6 blue squares. Take turns.

Try Pick a tile. Say the difference next to that number. Do you see a subtraction problem with that difference on the game board?

If **YES**, cover it with a square.

If **NO**, lose your turn.
Put the tile back in the 🛍.

87 – 40	85 – 20	88 – 50
94 – 20	98 – 60	97 – 50
93 – 10	86 – 30	96 – 40

⌐1⌐	The difference is 38.
⌐2⌐	The difference is 47.
⌐3⌐	The difference is 56.
⌐4⌐	The difference is 65.
⌐5⌐	The difference is 74.
⌐6⌐	The difference is 83.

To win, get: ■ ■ ■ or ■ or ■ or ■
               ■   ■   ■
               ■   ■   ■

Try Again Tell a subtraction story with the numbers in each space on the game board.

Look and See

Start 👥 Get 14 red squares. Cover every number in each column with a square. Take turns.

Try Uncover one number in each column. Did you get two parts of 100? Use the ten-frames to explain your answer.

If your answer is **YES**, keep the squares.

If your answer is **NO**, put the squares back.

43		44
75		36
29		71
64		83
56		57
17		62
38		25

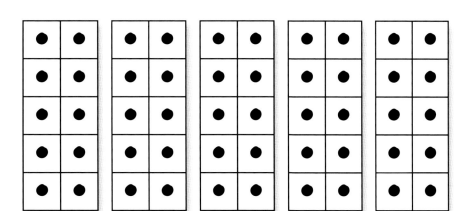

Take turns until every number is uncovered.

Try Again Cover every number. Play again!

Look and See

Partner Talk

Share your thinking while you work.

Start Put 0 1 2 3 4 5 6 7 8 9 in a .

Take turns.

Try Pick two tiles. Show a two-digit number in the spaces on the left.
Tell your partner how to find the other part of 100.
Use the ten-frames. Repeat until the is empty.

Try Again This time, say an addition sentence that
has your two parts of 100.

Helping Hands

Start 👫 Get 8 red squares. Take turns.

Try Pick a snail. Tell your partner how to subtract those numbers on the hundred chart. Find and cover the difference on a flower below. Take turns until every difference is covered.

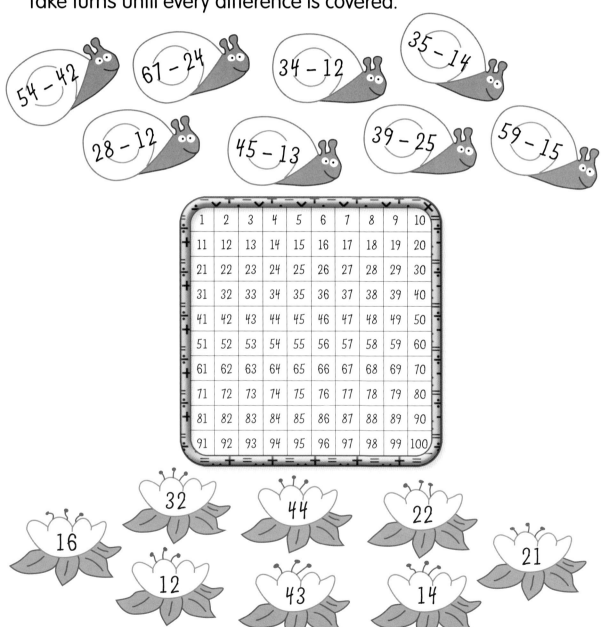

54 – 42   67 – 24   34 – 12   35 – 14

28 – 12   45 – 13   39 – 25   59 – 15

1	2	3	4	5	6	7	8	9	10
11	12	13	14	15	16	17	18	19	20
21	22	23	24	25	26	27	28	29	30
31	32	33	34	35	36	37	38	39	40
41	42	43	44	45	46	47	48	49	50
51	52	53	54	55	56	57	58	59	60
61	62	63	64	65	66	67	68	69	70
71	72	73	74	75	76	77	78	79	80
81	82	83	84	85	86	87	88	89	90
91	92	93	94	95	96	97	98	99	100

16   32   44   22   21

12   43   14

Try Again Remove the squares. Point to a number below the chart. Ask your partner to find two numbers with that difference.

Helping Hands

Partner Talk

Share your thinking while you work.

Start 👫 Get 10 red squares. Work together.

Try Look at the subtraction problems in each row.
Find two that have the same difference.
Cover them with red squares.

55 – 23	89 – 24	57 – 21	78 – 13
47 – 16	38 – 17	67 – 27	77 – 46
49 – 32	85 – 14	44 – 21	91 – 20
38 – 12	47 – 21	77 – 41	79 – 36
75 – 22	65 – 43	98 – 45	45 – 24

1	2	3	4	5	6	7	8	9	10
11	12	13	14	15	16	17	18	19	20
21	22	23	24	25	26	27	28	29	30
31	32	33	34	35	36	37	38	39	40
41	42	43	44	45	46	47	48	49	50
51	52	53	54	55	56	57	58	59	60
61	62	63	64	65	66	67	68	69	70
71	72	73	74	75	76	77	78	79	80
81	82	83	84	85	86	87	88	89	90
91	92	93	94	95	96	97	98	99	100

Try Again This time, talk about the two problems in each row
that do not have the same difference.
Use the hundred chart to find each difference.

Partner Talk
Share your thinking while you work.

Try Together

Start 👥 Get 15 red squares. Take turns.

Try Start with a number in the center of a flower. Choose one of the numbers around it. Add on to find the difference. Cover the difference below. Take turns until every difference is covered.

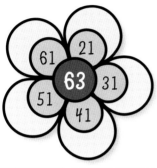

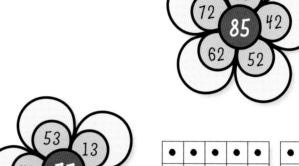

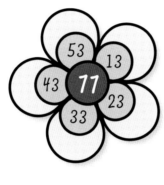

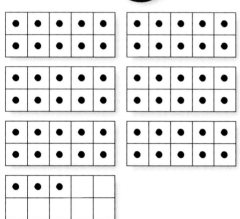

22	44	2	64	32
54	23	13	12	24
33	53	42	34	43

Try Again Remove the squares. Try again!

Try Together

Start 👫 Get ☐1 ☐2 ☐3 . Get 12 red squares. Take turns.

Try Point to the number on a flower pot.
Use tiles to make a two-digit number here.
Subtract it from the one on the flower pot. Add
on to find the difference. Use a square to cover
the difference on a flower.
Repeat until every flower is covered.

Subtract

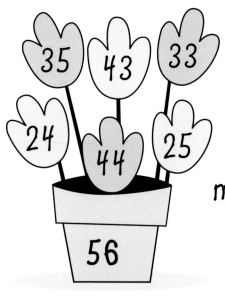

Use
mental math
to solve!

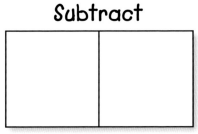

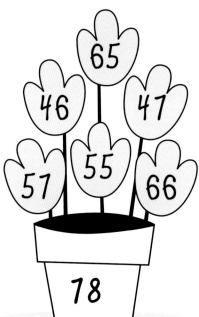

Try Again Remove the squares. Begin again!

Try Together

Partner Talk

Share your thinking while you work.

Start Get 1 2 3 4 5 6 7 8 9 . Get 4 red squares.

Try Read a problem. Can you solve it?
If not, place a square to point to **NO**, and explain why you cannot solve the problem.
If you can, place a square to point to **YES**, and then use number tiles to solve it.

a. 6 ducks are swimming in the pond.
2 ducks leave the water.
How many are still swimming?

 **YES   NO**

b. Mother Bird has 4 eggs in her nest.
Some have begun to hatch. How many have not begun to hatch?

YES   NO

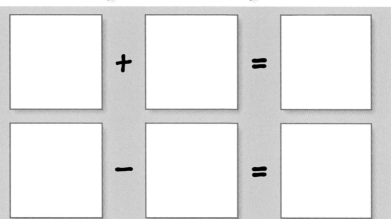

c. Mr. Squirrel hid 7 nuts under a tree.
He forgot where he hid some. How many nuts did he dig up?

 **YES   NO**

d. 5 bunnies are eating carrots. 2 more bunnies join them. How many bunnies are there altogether?

 **YES   NO**

Try Again Play again! This time, choose your own numbers for the missing information in problems **b** and **c**.

Try Together

Partner Talk

Share your thinking while you work.

Start 👥 Get

1 1 2 2 3 3 4 4 5 5 6 6 7 7 8 8 9 9. Get 4 🖇 and 5 red squares.

Try Read a problem. Can you solve it?
If not, place a square to point to **NO**, and explain why you cannot solve the problem.
If you can, place a square to point to **YES**, and then use number tiles to solve it. If there is extra information, use a 🖇 to cover it.

a. Jan drives 2 miles to the store. Her car has 4 windows. She drives another mile to the library. How many miles does Jan drive?

YES

NO

b. Tammy's coat has 6 buttons. Some of the buttons fell off. How many buttons are still on the coat?

YES   NO

c. Nine children are at the park. The park has 4 swings. 3 children are playing soccer. How many children are not playing soccer?

YES

NO

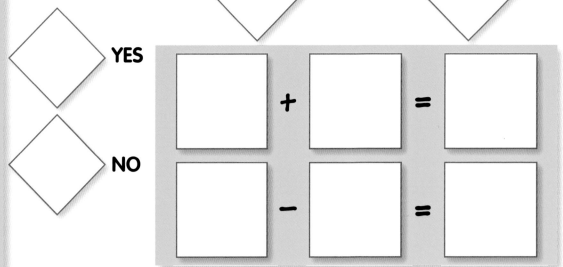

d. Four butterflies are in the garden. Some land on flowers. How many are still flying?

YES   NO

e. Bill's book has 8 pages. The book is about fish. He reads 6 pages. How many pages are left?

YES   NO

Try Again This time, choose your own numbers for the missing information.

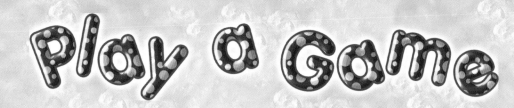

Partner Talk

Share your thinking while you work.

Start (🚶) Get a 🎲. Get 11 red squares. Get 20 blue squares. Give one game board to each player. Take turns.

Try Toss the 🎲. Collect that number of blue squares. Put them in your ones place. Each blue square is worth 1 point. If you have 10 or more ones, trade 10 blue squares for a red square. Each red square is worth 10 points. Put a red square in the tens place. Say your score.

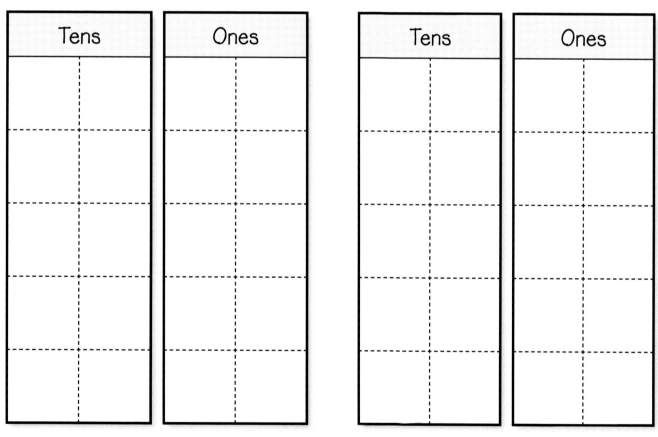

Tens	Ones

Player 1

Tens	Ones

Player 2

To win, be the first player to get 60 or more points.

Try Again Play again!

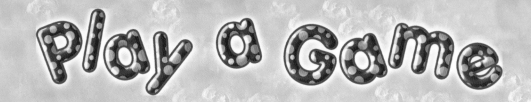

Partner Talk

Share your thinking while you work.

Start  Put 0 1 2 3 4 5 6 7 8 9 in a 🛍.

Get 17 red squares. Get 20 blue squares.
Give one game board to each player. Take turns.

Try Pick a tile. Collect that number of blue squares. Put them in your ones place. Each blue square is worth 1 point. If you have 10 or more ones, trade 10 blue squares for a red square. Each red square is worth 10 points. Put a red square in the tens place. Say your score. Put the tile back in the 🛍.

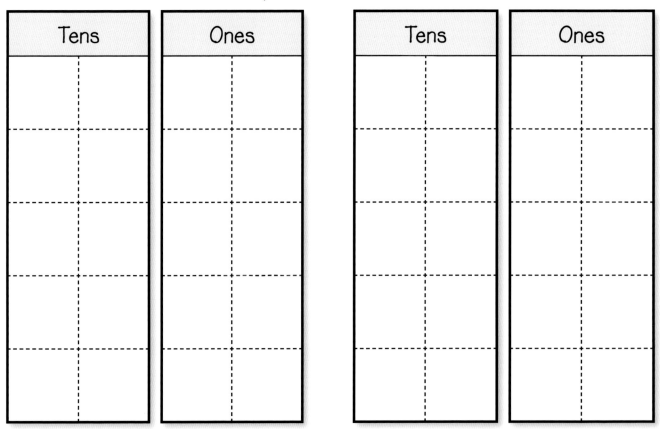

Tens	Ones		Tens	Ones

Player 1   Player 2

To win, be the first player to get 90 or more points.

Try Again Play again!

Listen and Learn

Partner Talk

Share your thinking while you work.

Start 🏃 Put ①②③④⑤⑥⑦⑧⑨ in a .

Take turns until the 🛍 is empty.

Try Pick a tile. Place it in the first puzzle. Work together. Do you need to regroup? Find the sum. Move your tile to another puzzle. Tell if you need to regroup. Try each puzzle.

tens	ones
2	4
	⬜
+	

Regroup? Yes or No?

tens	ones
7	6
	⬜
+	

Regroup? Yes or No?

tens	ones
1	8
	⬜
+	

Regroup? Yes or No?

tens	ones
3	5
	⬜
+	

Regroup? Yes or No?

Try Again Put the tiles back in the 🛍. Choose your own two-digit number. Take turns picking tiles. Each time you pick a tile, decide if you have to regroup to add that number to your number.

Listen and Learn

Partner Talk

Share your thinking while you work.

Start 👤 Get 1 2 3 4 5 6 7 8 9 . Work together.

Try Choose a puzzle. Place two tiles to solve that puzzle. Explain why your answer is correct. Ask your partner to find a different way to complete the puzzle. Try every puzzle.

tens	ones
3	4
+	
3	

tens	ones
2	7
+	
3	

tens	ones
4	3
+	
4	

tens	ones
7	5
+	
8	

Try Again In which puzzles do you have to regroup? How do you know?

Try Together

Partner Talk

Share your thinking while you work.

Start Put 2 3 4 5 6 7 8 9 in a .

Take turns.

Try Pick a tile. Look at every puzzle. Decide where that tile belongs.
Put it there. Tell your partner why that number belongs there.

tens	ones
1	5
+ 3	1

tens	ones
1	8
+ 1	9

tens	ones
5	7
+ 2	8

tens	ones
5	4
+ 3	9

Continue until you have one tile in each space.

Try Again Take turns. Make up an addition problem.
Ask your partner to show the answer with tiles.

Center Activity 8-3 ★   Topic 8   **5**

Try Together

Start  Put ⟨2⟩ ⟨3⟩ ⟨4⟩ ⟨5⟩ ⟨6⟩ ⟨7⟩ ⟨8⟩ ⟨9⟩ in a .

Take turns.

Try Pick a tile. Look at every puzzle. Decide where that tile belongs. Put it there. Tell your partner why that number belongs there.

tens	ones
2	5
+	
9	9

tens	ones
4	5
+	
8	0

tens	ones
	9
+	
9	1

tens	ones
1	4
+	
8	3

Continue until you have one tile in each space.

Try Again Make up a puzzle like this one.
Ask your partner to show the answer with tiles.

Look and See

Start 👤 Get

Work together.

Try Choose two towers. Use the tiles to show the number of blocks in each tower. How many blocks does it take to build both towers?

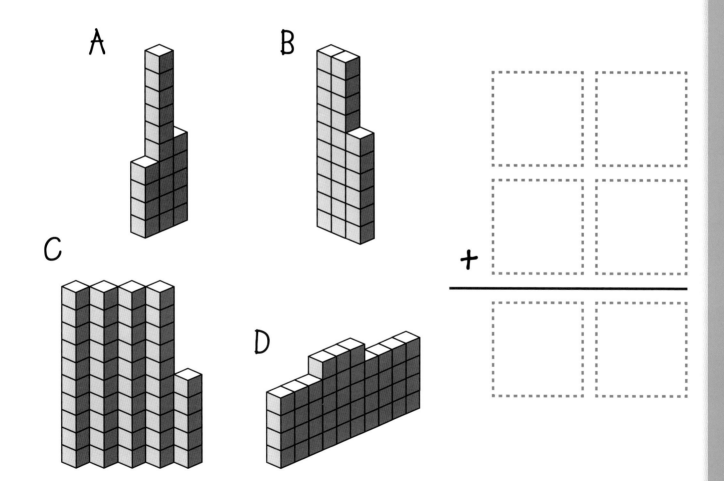

A   B

C

D

+

Try Again Work together until you make six different addition problems.

Look and See

Partner Talk

Share your thinking while you work.

Start 🏃 Get

0 0 1 1 2 2 3 3 4 4
5 5 6 6 7 7 8 8 9 9 .

Try Choose a number in a circle.
Which two towers are built with that number of blocks?

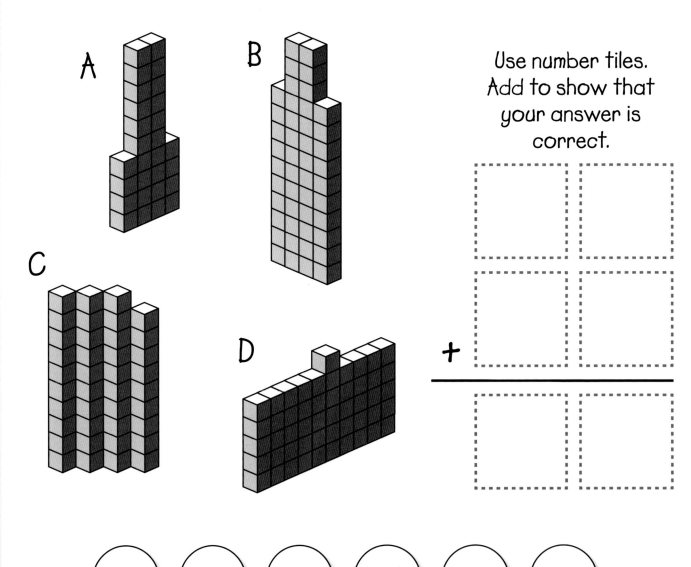

A

B

C

D

Use number tiles.
Add to show that
your answer is
correct.

+

79 74 67 85 97 90

Try Again Repeat for every number.

Share your thinking while you work.

Start 🚶 Get a 🎲. Get 0 1 2 3 4 5 6 7 8 9.

Get 7 blue squares for one player.
Get 7 red squares for the other player.

Try Toss the 🎲. Find your toss below.
Use tiles to explain how to add
those numbers. Cover the sum if you
see it on the game board.

Display Tiles Here

 64 + 15

⚀ 78 + 15

⚁ 31 + 29

⚂ 25 + 39

⚃ 53 + 14

⚄ 54 + 37

+

67	60	64	93
91	93	79	67
79	64	60	91

To win, be the first to
cover 7 spaces.

Try Again Play again! For which tosses do you need to regroup?

Play a Game

Partner Talk

Share your thinking while you work.

Start 🎲 Get a 🎲. Get  ⓪ ① ② ③ ④ ⑤ ⑥ ⑦ ⑧ ⑨.

Get 7 blue squares for one player.
Get 7 red squares for the other player.

Try Toss the 🎲. Find your toss below. Display tiles for the numbers next to your dots. Find the missing number. Cover the missing number if you see it on the game board.

Display Tiles Here

⚀ $36 + \square\square = 90$

⚁ $63 + \square\square = 82$

⚂ $43 + \square\square = 68$

⚃ $38 + \square\square = 94$

⚄ $26 + \square\square = 71$

⚅ $58 + \square\square = 90$

45	54	32	25
19	25	19	56
56	32	54	45

To win, be the first to cover 7 spaces.

Try Again Play again! For which tosses do you need to regroup?

Center Activity 8-5 ⭐ ⭐

Try Together

Start 👫 Get ⓪ ① ② ③ ④ ⑤ ⑥ ⑦ ⑧ ⑨.

Work together.

Try Choose a puzzle. Explain how to add the numbers.
Ask your partner to add those numbers in a different way.
Use number tiles to show your answer.

$$
\begin{array}{r}
1\ 8 \\
7 \\
+\ 1\ 4 \\
\hline
\end{array}
\qquad
\begin{array}{r}
1\ 6 \\
9 \\
+\ 2\ 2 \\
\hline
\end{array}
\qquad
\begin{array}{r}
1\ 2 \\
3\ 3 \\
+\ 1\ 7 \\
\hline
\end{array}
$$

$$
\begin{array}{r}
2\ 1 \\
2\ 2 \\
+\ \ \ 7 \\
\hline
\end{array}
\qquad
\begin{array}{r}
4\ 7 \\
2\ 4 \\
+\ 1\ 0 \\
\hline
\end{array}
$$

Complete every puzzle. Use each tile once.

Try Again Make up a puzzle about adding three numbers.
Ask your partner to show the answer with tiles.

Try Together

Partner
Talk

Share your thinking while you work.

Start 👥 Get ⓪ ① ② ③ ④ ⑤ ⑥ ⑦ ⑧ ⑨ .

Work together. Complete every puzzle. Use each tile once.

Try Choose a puzzle. Explain how to find the missing number.
Show that number with tiles. To check your answer,
add the three numbers in two different ways.

```
   2  1          3  6          □  □
   1  2          □  □          1  8
   □             9             3  1
+ ___        + _____      + _____
   4  2          6  5          9  5
```

```
   5  4          3  3          1  3
      8             □          5  2
   □  □          2            □  □
+ _____     + _____     + _____
   9  9          1  4          8  3
                 7  2
```

Try Again Make up a puzzle like one of these.
Ask your partner to show the answer with tiles.

Look and See

Partner Talk

Share your thinking while you work.

 Get 15 red squares. Get 15 blue squares. Take turns.

Try Read a problem. Think about how you want to solve it. Choose a picture, a number sentence, or use squares on the workmat. Explain. Say the answer. Then ask your partner to solve the problem in a different way.

a. Marcia went for a nature walk in the woods. She saw 13 maple trees and 12 oak trees. How many trees did she see in all?

$$\begin{array}{r} 13 \\ + 12 \\ \hline \end{array}$$

$13 + 12 = \square$

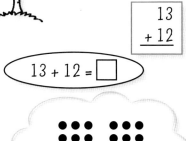

b. The restaurant served 15 hamburgers during lunch time. They served another 10 hamburgers in the afternoon. How many blocks in all are in the tower?

$$\begin{array}{r} 15 \\ + 10 \\ \hline \end{array}$$

$15 + 10 = \square$

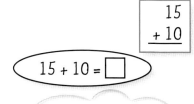

c. Joe and Nica are jumping rope. Joe jumps 16 times. Nica jumps 16 times. How many jumps is that altogether?

$$\begin{array}{r} 16 \\ + 16 \\ \hline \end{array}$$

$16 + 16 = \square$

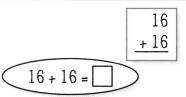

WORKMAT

PART	PART

Try Again Make up a different problem that you can solve with one of the pictures above the workmat.

Look and See

Partner Talk

Share your thinking while you work.

Start  Get 20 red squares. Get 20 blue squares. Take turns.

Try Read a problem. Think about how you want to solve it. Choose a picture, a number sentence, or use squares on the workmat. Explain. Say the answer. Then ask your partner to solve the problem in a different way.

a. On Monday, Sue counted 19 flowers blooming in the garden. On Thursday, she counted another 18 flowers blooming. How many flowers are now blooming in the garden?

b. Mikey uses 14 blocks to make a tower. His friend Matt adds 17 more blocks to the tower. How many blocks in all are in the tower?

c. Grandma is baking nut bread. She adds 15 nuts to the mix. Then she makes another nut bread with the same number of nuts. How many nuts are in both nut breads?

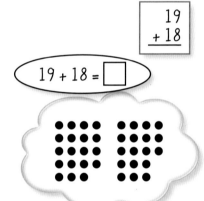

$$\begin{array}{r} 19 \\ + 18 \\ \hline \end{array}$$

$19 + 18 = \boxed{}$

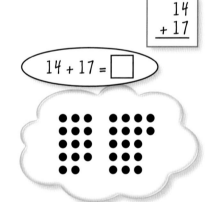

$$\begin{array}{r} 14 \\ + 17 \\ \hline \end{array}$$

$14 + 17 = \boxed{}$

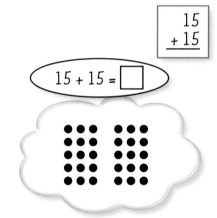

$$\begin{array}{r} 15 \\ + 15 \\ \hline \end{array}$$

$15 + 15 = \boxed{}$

WORKMAT

PART   PART

Try Again Make up a different problem that you can solve with one of the number sentences on this page.

Center Activity 8-7 ⭐ ⭐

Look and See

Partner Talk

Share your thinking while you work.

Start  Put ①②③④⑤⑥⑦⑧⑨ in a .

Get 30 squares. Take turns until you use all the circles.

Try Pick a number in a circle. Show that number of squares on the workmat. Ask your partner to pick a tile. Subtract that number of squares.

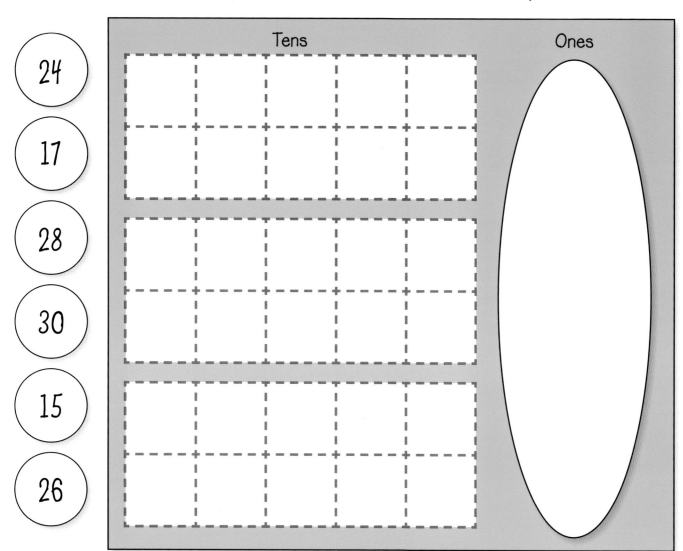

24

17

28

30

15

26

Tens   Ones

Did you need to regroup? Why or why not?

Try Again Put the tile back in the 🛍. Remove the squares. Try again!

Look and See

Partner Talk

Share your thinking while you work.

Start 👫 Put ①②③④⑤⑥⑦⑧⑨ in a 🛍.

Get 30 squares. Take turns until you use all the circles.

Try Pick a number in a circle.
Show that number of squares on the workmat.
Ask your partner to pick a tile. Subtract that number of squares.

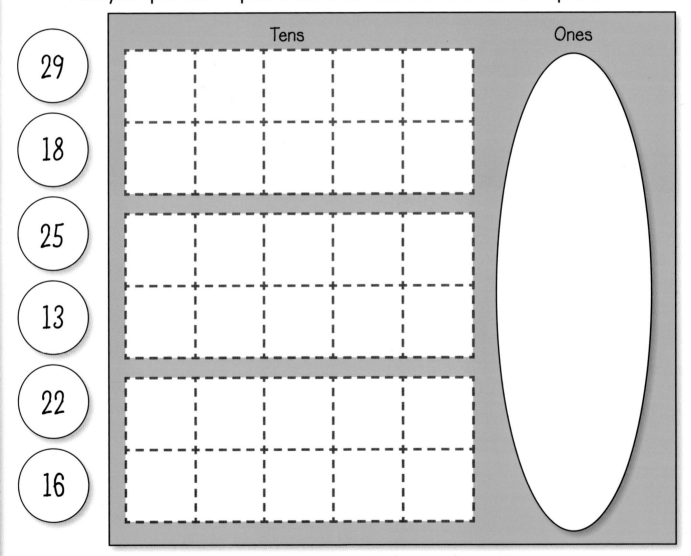

Tens   Ones

29
18
25
13
22
16

Did you need to regroup? Why or why not?

Try Again Put the tile back in the 🛍. Remove the squares. Try again!

Center Activity 9-1 ⭐⭐

Share your thinking while you work.

Try Together

Start  Put 1 2 3 4 5 6 7 8 9 in a 🛍.

Take turns.

Try Pick a tile. Explain how to subtract that number from 24, 70, 42, and 31. Set the tile aside. Repeat until the 🛍 is empty.

tens	ones
2	4
−	

Regroup?
Yes   No

tens	ones
7	0
−	

Regroup?
Yes   No

tens	ones
4	2
−	

Regroup?
Yes   No

tens	ones
3	1
−	

Regroup?
Yes   No

Try Again Put the tiles back in the 🛍. Play again.

Try Together

Partner Talk

Share your thinking while you work.

Start ✿ Get ⓪ ① ② ③ ④ ⑤ ⑥ ⑦ ⑧ ⑨ .

Try Choose a puzzle. Solve the puzzle with tiles. Explain why your difference is correct. Did you need to regroup? Why or why not? Solve the puzzle in a different way. Repeat for each puzzle.

tens	ones
3	7
−	
3	

tens	ones
2	3
−	
1	

tens	ones
4	9
−	
4	

tens	ones
7	2
−	
6	

Try Again This time, find four different ways to solve each puzzle.

4 Topic 9 **Center Activity 9-2** ★ ★

Play a Game

Partner Talk

Share your thinking while you work.

Start Put 1 2 3 4 5 6 7 8 9 in a 🛍.

Get 18 red squares.
Give one game board to each player.
Take turns.

tens	ones
5	3
−	

Regroup?
Yes   No

Try Pick a tile. Put it in the ones place in the place value chart. Explain how to subtract that number from 53. Do you need to regroup? If you see the difference on your game board, cover it. Put the tile back in the 🛍.

Remember to regroup if you need to!

Four Corners

51	47	49
46	52	44
45	48	50

Four Corners

44	51	52
49	48	46
47	50	45

To win, be the first player who covers four corners.

Try Again Play again! Which numbers can you subtract without regrouping?

Play a Game

Partner Talk

Share your thinking while you work.

Start 👥 Put 1 2 3 4 5 6 7 8 9 in a 🛍️.

Get 18 red squares.
Give one game board to each player.
Take turns.

tens	ones
8	1

Try Pick a tile. Put it in the ones place in the place value chart. Explain how to subtract that number from 81. Do you need to regroup? If you see your difference on your game board, cover it. Put the tile back in the 🛍️.

Remember to regroup if you need to!

Regroup?
Yes   No

Four Corners

76	74	79
75	80	72
78	73	77

Four Corners

80	78	73
72	79	77
74	76	75

To win, be the first player who covers four corners.

Try Again Play again! Talk about why most of the numbers in the game board have 7 tens.

Look and See

Start 👥 Get 34 squares. Put them on the workmat. Take turns.

Try Pick a number in a circle.
Talk with your partner. Answer this question:
"Do you need to regroup to subtract that number of squares?"

24

17

28

30

26

15

Tens	Ones

After you find the difference,
say a subtraction sentence that has your difference.

Try Again Make sure all 34 squares are on the workmat.
Repeat until you use all the circles.

Look and See

Partner Talk

Share your thinking while you work.

Start 👥 Get 32 squares. Put them on the workmat.

Try Take turns picking a number in a circle. Every time you pick a number, answer this question: "Do you need to regroup to subtract that number of squares from those on the workmat?" Explain why or why not. Find the difference.

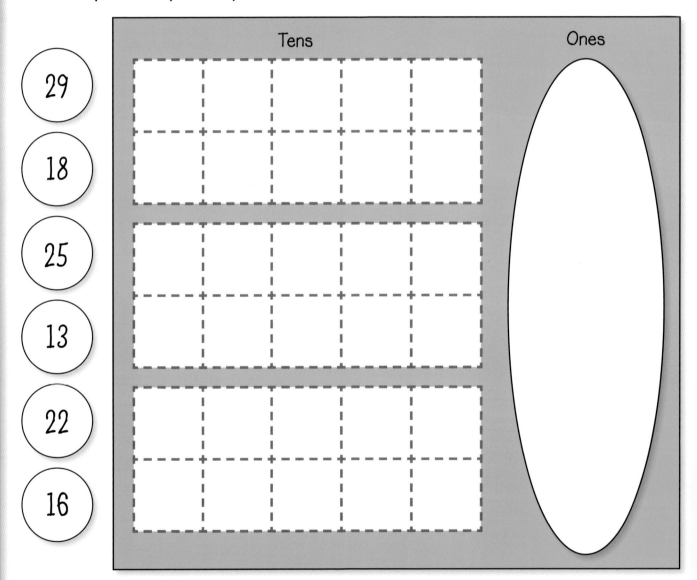

Try Again What if each number in a circle is a difference? What number would you subtract from 32 to get that difference?

Center Activity 9-4 ⭐ ⭐

Cover Three

Start 👥 Get 9 red squares. Cover the subtraction problems.
Get 6 red squares for one player. Get 6 blue squares for
the other player. Get ✏️. Take turns.

Try Uncover a subtraction problem. Use paper and a pencil to subtract.
Look for the difference on the game board, and cover it with a square.

38 – 16

58 – 33

72 – 12

44 – 21

65 – 16

41 – 28

88 – 44

63 – 29

56 – 44

44	25	34
12	23	60
13	49	22

To win, be the first player who gets 3 game spaces
with connected sides. Look for these ways to win.

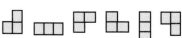

Try Again Play again!

Cover Three

Partner Talk

Share your thinking while you work.

Start Get 9 red squares. Cover the differences.
Get 6 red squares for one player. Get 6 blue squares for the other player. Get . Take turns.

Try Uncover a difference. Look on the game board for two numbers that have the difference you uncovered. Explain how to subtract. Cover those numbers.

60

39

17

8

13

62

41

29

35

85 – 46	60 – 31	77 – 17
94 – 59	91 – 29	40 – 27
46 – 38	64 – 47	58 – 17

To win, be the first player who gets 3 game spaces with connected sides. Look for these ways to win.

Try Again Choose a difference. Make up another subtraction sentence that has that difference.

 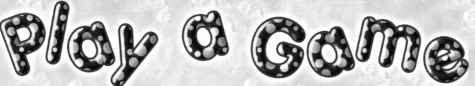 

Start  Get 12 red squares.
Cover each game space with a square.
Take turns.

Try Uncover two game spaces.

If you see a subtraction problem and a way to check the answer by adding, keep the squares.

If not, put the squares back where they were.

Take turns until all the spaces are uncovered.

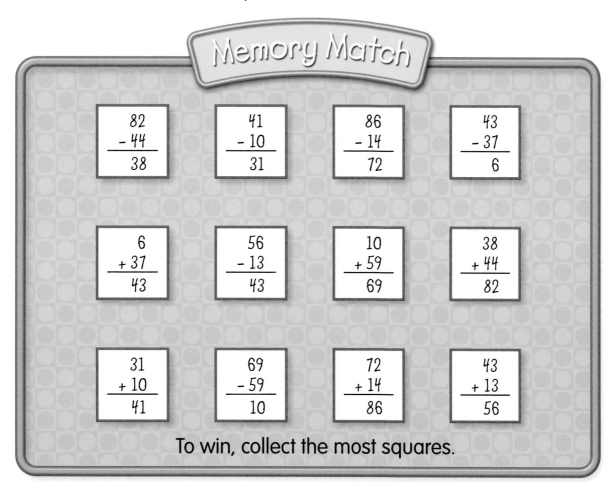

Memory Match

82 − 44 = 38	41 − 10 = 31	86 − 14 = 72	43 − 37 = 6
6 + 37 = 43	56 − 13 = 43	10 + 59 = 69	38 + 44 = 82
31 + 10 = 41	69 − 59 = 10	72 + 14 = 86	43 + 13 = 56

To win, collect the most squares.

Try Again Play again!

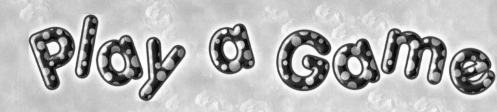

Partner Talk

Share your thinking while you work.

Start Get 12 red squares.
Cover each game space with a square.
Take turns.

Try Uncover two game spaces.

If you see a subtraction problem and a way to check the answer by adding, keep the squares.

If not, put the squares back where they were.

Take turns until all the spaces are uncovered.

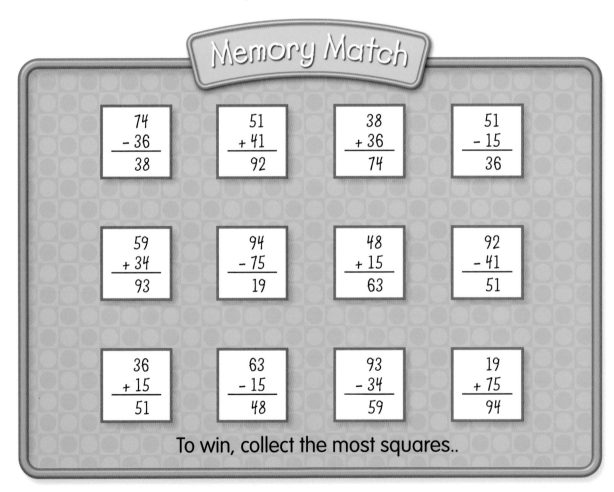

Memory Match

74 − 36 38	51 + 41 92	38 + 36 74	51 − 15 36
59 + 34 93	94 − 75 19	48 + 15 63	92 − 41 51
36 + 15 51	63 − 15 48	93 − 34 59	19 + 75 94

To win, collect the most squares..

Try Again Play again! This time make your own game board.

Look and See

Partner Talk
Share your thinking while you work.

Start  Get 20 red squares. Get 20 blue squares. Get   . Work together.

Try Read a two-question problem. To answer the first question, put squares on the workmat. Then find the number sentence with those numbers. Put a ⬭ on it. Do the same for the second question.

a. Kelly and Tom go apple picking. Kelly picks 12 apples and Tom picked 10 apples. How many do they pick altogether?

At home, they use 14 of the apples to make a pie. How many apples are left?

b. There are 17 children playing at the park. 11 of them leave. How many children are left at the park?

Then 9 other children come to the park. How many are at the park altogether?

17 – 11 = ☐

13 + 16 = ☐

6 + 9 = ☐

c. Sally and Patty collect bookmarks. Sally has 16 bookmarks. Patty has 3 less than Sally. How many does Patty have?

How many bookmarks do Sally and Patty have altogether?

16 – 3 = ☐

22 – 14 = ☐

12 + 10 = ☐

WORKMAT

Try Again Change the numbers in one of the problems. Work together to solve the problem again.

Look and See

Start  Get 20 red squares. Get 20 blue squares.

Get 2 sets of 0 1 2 3 4 5 6 7 8 9.

Take turns.

Try Read a two-question problem to your group. To answer the first question, use squares on the workmat. Then make a number sentence with tiles. Do the same for the second question.

a. Ron does 15 push-ups on Friday. On Saturday, he does 4 more than on Friday. How many push-ups did he do on Saturday? One month later, Ron does twice as many push-ups. How many push-ups is he doing one month later?

b. At snack time, Ms. Green shares 12 oatmeal cookies and 23 raisin cookies with her class. How many cookies are there altogether? The children eat 23 of them. How many cookies are left?

c. Jenny is making a necklace with blue and pink beads. She gets 21 blue beads and 19 pink beads. How many beads does she have? If she gives 25 of the beads to her sister, how many beads does each girl have?

 + or −  =

WORKMAT

Try Again This time, change the numbers in one of the problems. Or, make a two-part problem for your group to solve.

Look and See

Partner Talk
Share your thinking while you work.

Start  Get 10 red squares.

Get  0 1 2 3 4 5 6 7 8 9

and 0 1 2 3 4 5 6 7 8 9 .

Take turns until each partner gets 5 turns.

Try Point to the prices for two school supplies. Use number tiles to add those amounts of money. Find a pocket that has the money you need to buy those school supplies. Cover it with a square. If you cannot find a pocket to cover, your turn is over.

Add Here

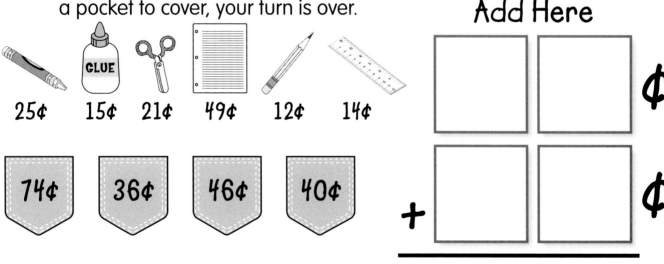

25¢   15¢   21¢   49¢   12¢   14¢

74¢   36¢   46¢   40¢

39¢   37¢   27¢   33¢

29¢   61¢   35¢   64¢   70¢   63¢   26¢

Try Again Begin again! Tell why it is important to put the cent symbol after the sum.

Look and See

Start  Get 16 red squares.

Get ⓪ ① ② ③ ④ ⑤ ⑥ ⑦ ⑧ ⑨

and ⓪ ① ② ③ ④ ⑤ ⑥ ⑦ ⑧ ⑨ .

Take turns until every toy is covered.

Add Here

Try Point to a purse. Tell how much money you have. Pick two toys. Add the two amounts of money using tiles. If you have enough money to buy both toys, cover those toys with squares.
If not, miss your turn.

¢

+

¢

¢

Start 👫 Put  in a 🛍️.

Take turns.

Try Pick a tile. Show it in the tens place to make a number next to the cent sign. Talk with your partner.

Do you have enough money to buy the toys on the top shelf?
Do you have enough money to buy the toys on the middle shelf?
Do you have enough money to buy the toys on the bottom shelf?

Repeat until the 🛍️ is empty.

Try Again This time, see if you have enough money to buy the three toys on the left side, or the three on the right side.

Try Together

Start 👤 Put  3 4 5 6 7 8 9 in a 🛍️ .

Take turns.

Try Pick a tile. Show it in the tens place to make a number next to the cent sign. Talk with your partner. Which two toys can you buy with the money you have?

Repeat until the 🛍️ is empty.

Try Again This time, decide if you have enough money for three toys.

Try Together

Start  Get ⌊0⌋ ⌊1⌋ ⌊2⌋ ⌊3⌋ ⌊4⌋ ⌊5⌋ ⌊6⌋ ⌊7⌋ ⌊8⌋ ⌊9⌋

and ⌊0⌋ ⌊1⌋ ⌊2⌋ ⌊3⌋ ⌊4⌋ ⌊5⌋ ⌊6⌋ ⌊7⌋ ⌊8⌋ ⌊9⌋ .

Get a ⌒. Get 10 red squares. Get ✎.
Cover each mitten with a red square. Work together.

Try Uncover two mittens. Put tiles in the spaces to show the numbers you will add. Talk about how you will add. Put the ⌒ below the method you choose. Show the sum. Play until every mitten is uncovered.

Choose

Mental Math   Paper and pencil

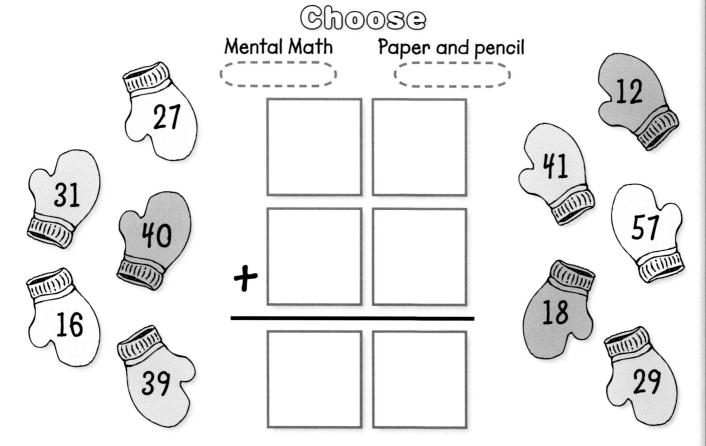

Try Again Look at a snowball. It has a sum of two numbers that are on the mittens. Can you find which mittens?

72 60 47
30 56 49

Partner
Talk

Share your thinking while you work.

Start 👥 Get a 🎲. Get ✏️.

Get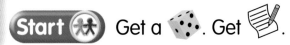

and 0 1 2 3 4 5 6 7 8 9.

Take turns until each partner gets 5 turns.

Try Toss the 🎲. Find your toss in the chart.
Read the directions for your toss.

Toss • ⚁ ⚂	Toss ⚃ ⚄ ⚅
Use tiles to make an addition problem your partner will solve with mental math.	Use tiles to make an addition problem your partner will solve with paper and a pencil.

You do not always
need a pencil.
Try mental math!

Try Again Take turns. Use two tiles to show a sum. Ask your partner
to show two numbers that have the sum you chose.

Look and See

Partner Talk
Share your thinking while you work.

Start 🚶 Get a ✏️ and a 📎 to make a 🔄.

Get 0 1 2 3 4 5 6 7 8 9

and 0 1 2 3 4 5 6 7 8 9 . Take turns.

Choose **A** or **B**. Spin to show how much money you have. Point to a car you can buy. Use tiles to show the subtraction problem for your numbers. Tell how much money you have left. Each player gets four turns.

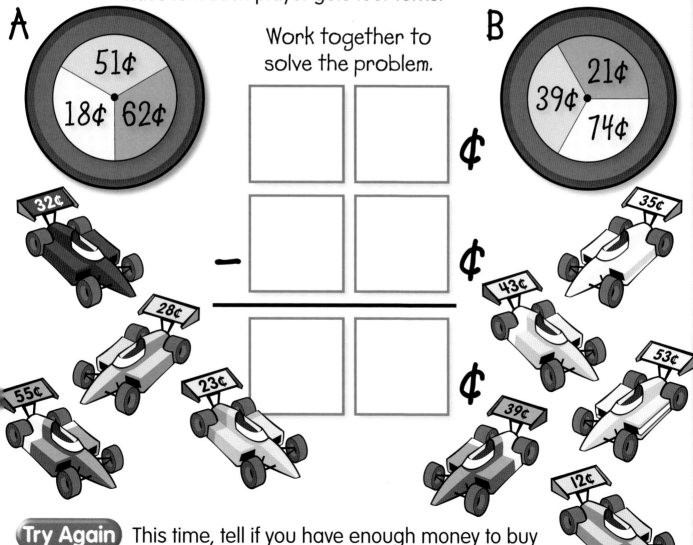

A — 51¢ 18¢ 62¢

Work together to solve the problem.

B — 21¢ 39¢ 74¢

32¢ 28¢ 55¢ 23¢ 35¢ 43¢ 53¢ 39¢ 12¢

Try Again This time, tell if you have enough money to buy another car. Tell your partner which one.

Center Activity 10-4 ⭐   Topic 10   **7**

Look and See

Partner Talk

Share your thinking while you work.

Start 👤 Get a 🎲. Get 0 1 2 3 4 5 6 7 8 9
and 0 1 2 3 4 5 6 7 8 9.

Take turns.

Try Toss the 🎲 to find the amount of money you have. Choose a toy you can buy. Use tiles to show the subtraction problem. Solve that problem. Tell how much money you have left. Each player gets four turns.

⚀ 75¢   ⚁ 59¢   ⚂ 97¢

⚃ 82¢   ⚄ 84¢   ⚅ 67¢

Work together to solve the problem.

¢

─

¢

───

¢

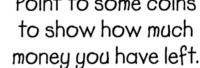

72¢

56¢

32¢

65¢

24¢

85¢

91¢

Point to some coins to show how much money you have left.

Try Again Play again! This time, tell if you have enough money left to buy another toy.

Try Together

Partner Talk

Share your thinking while you work.

Start  Put ⁴ ⁵ ⁶ ⁷ ⁸ ⁹ in a 🛍.

Get 18 red squares and 6 blue squares. Take turns.

Try Pick two tiles and place them in the hand.
Show how many dimes and pennies you have to spend.
Place red squares below the coins to help you count.

Now pick a toy. Tell whether you will have more or less than 20¢ left after you buy that toy. Cover that toy with a blue square.

Try Again Put the tiles back in the . Repeat until all the toys are covered.

Try Together

Partner Talk
Share your thinking while you work.

Start 👥 Put  4 5 6 7 8 9 in a 🛍.

Get 18 red squares and 6 blue squares. Take turns.

Try Pick two tiles and place them in the hand.
Show how many dimes and pennies you have to spend.
Place red squares below the coins to help you count.

Now pick a snack. Tell whether you will have more or less than 20¢ left after you buy that snack. Cover that snack with a blue square.

Drink 36¢ popcorn 42¢ 15¢
28¢ Raisins 25¢ Peanuts 19¢

Try Again Put the tiles back in the . This time, buy two snacks if you have enough money in your hand. About how much money do you have left?

Try Together

Start  Get ⓪①②③④⑤⑥⑦⑧⑨

and ⓪①②③④⑤⑥⑦⑧⑨ .

Get 10 red squares. Use them to cover every balloon.

Get a ⚯ . Get ✎ . Work together.

Try Uncover a balloon. Say the subtraction problem. Put tiles in the spaces to show the numbers you will subtract. Talk about how you will subtract. Put the ⚯ below the method you choose. Show the difference. Play until every balloon is uncovered.

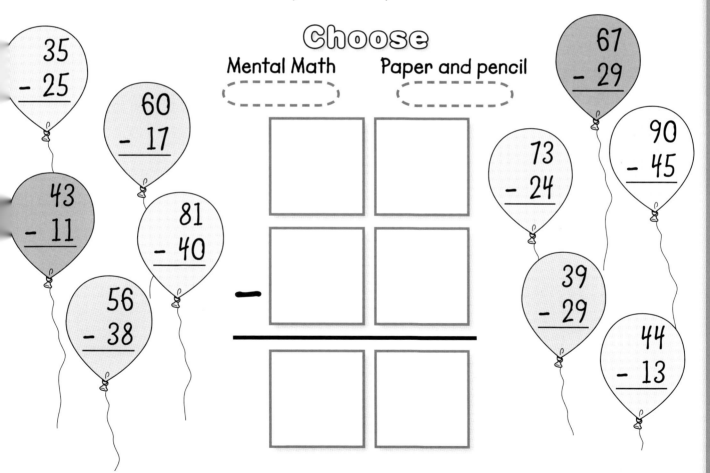

Choose

Mental Math   Paper and pencil

35 − 25

60 − 17

43 − 11

81 − 40

56 − 38

67 − 29

90 − 45

73 − 24

39 − 29

44 − 13

Try Again Begin again! This time, make up your own numbers for your partner to subtract. Tell your partner which method to use.

Center Activity 10-6 ⭐

Topic 10   **11**

Partner Talk

Share your thinking while you work.

Try Together

Start 👬 Get a 🎲. Get ✏️.

Get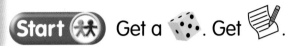

and **0 1 2 3 4 5 6 7 8 9**.

Take turns until each partner gets 5 turns.

Try Toss the 🎲. Find your toss in the chart.
Read the directions for your toss.

Toss ⚀ ⚁ ⚂	Toss ⚃ ⚄ ⚅
Use tiles to make a subtraction problem your partner will solve with mental math.	Use tiles to make a subtraction problem your partner will solve with paper and pencil.

You do not always need a pencil. Try mental math!

Try Again Take turns. Use two tiles to show a difference. Ask your partner to show two numbers that have the difference you chose.

Helping Hands

Start Get 0 1 2 3 4 5 6 7 8 9
and 0 1 2 3 4 5 6 7 8 9.

Work together.

Try Choose and read a problem.
Work together to solve it using tiles.
Try every problem.

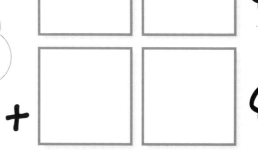

FRUIT	
apple	15¢
banana	12¢
peach	17¢
grapes	21¢
orange	18¢

TRY adding.
CHECK the sum.
REVISE if needed.

a. Jason buys two fruits. He pays 27¢ for them. Tell what he buys.

b. Myles buys two apples and one other fruit. The total is 42¢. Tell what the other fruit is.

c. Jacki buys grapes and a banana. Tell how much money she spends.

d. Gianna spends 38¢. Tell what she buys.

e. Gabriel has 35¢. He buys an orange. What else can he buy?

f. Tell how much money James needs if he buys two peaches.

Try Again Tell what TRY, CHECK, AND REVISE means.
Then, try to find three different answers for problem **e.**

Helping Hands

Partner Talk

Share your thinking while you work.

Start  Get ⬚0 ⬚1 ⬚2 ⬚3 ⬚4 ⬚5 ⬚6 ⬚7 ⬚8 ⬚9

and ⬚0 ⬚1 ⬚2 ⬚3 ⬚4 ⬚5 ⬚6 ⬚7 ⬚8 ⬚9 .

Work together.

Try Choose and read a problem. Solve it using tiles.

> TRY adding or subtracting.
> CHECK the sum or difference.
> REVISE if needed.

SEED PACKETS	
Watermelon	32¢
Corn	25¢
Bean	19¢
Tomato	27¢
Carrot	40¢

⬚ ⬚ ¢

+ or −

⬚ ⬚ ¢

⬚ ⬚ ¢

a. Suppose you have 96¢. You want to spend all your money on three seed packets of the same kind. Which kind can you buy?

b. You have 70¢. You buy two seed packets and receive 13¢ in change. Which packets did you buy?

c. Sue buys tomato packets. She also buys another seed packet. The total is 79¢. Tell what the other seed packet is.

d. Gianna spends 38¢. Tell which packets she buys.

e. Margaux has 50¢. She buys two seed packets and gets 4¢ in change. Tell which seed packets she buys.

f. Phil has 89¢. He wants to spend all the money on seed packets. Tell which packets he can buy.

Try Again This time, make up a story for your partner. Tell why it is sometimes necessary to use the TRY, CHECK AND REVISE method.

Start 👥 Get a 🎲.
Get 6 red squares for Player 1.
Get 6 blue squares for Player 2.
Give one game board to each player. Take turns.

Try Toss the 🎲. Find the shape next to that number
on your game board. Name that shape.
Read the fact about your shape to your partner.
Cover your shape. Lose your turn if your shape is already covered.

⚀		It has 12 edges.
⚁		It has 1 flat surface.
⚂		It has 2 flat surfaces.
⚃		It has 6 flat surfaces.
⚄		It has 5 flat surfaces.
⚅		It has 0 edges.

⚀		It has 5 vertices.
⚁		It has 0 vertices.
⚂		It has 0 flat surfaces.
⚃		It has 8 vertices.
⚄		It has 1 flat surface.
⚅		It has 12 edges.

To win, be first to cover every shape on your game board.

Try Again Play again!

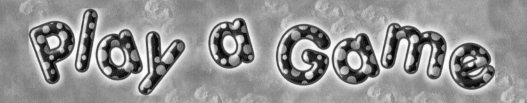

Start 🚶 Put 1 2 3 4 5 6 in a 🛍.

Get 12 red squares for Player 1. Get 12 blue squares for Player 2. Give one game board to each player. Take turns.

Try Pick a tile. Find the shape next to that number on your game board. Name that shape. Read one fact about your shape to your partner. Cover that fact. Lose your turn if both facts are already covered. Put the tile back in the 🛍.

1	It has 0 flat surfaces.	(sphere)	It has 0 edges.
2	It has 8 vertices.	(cube)	It has 6 flat surfaces.
3	It has 5 flat surfaces.	(pyramid)	It has 8 edges.
4	It has 12 edges.	(rectangular prism)	It has 8 vertices.
5	It has 2 flat surfaces.	(cylinder)	It has 0 edges.
6	It has 0 edges.	(cone)	It has 1 flat surface.

1	It has 0 edges.	(cone)	It has 1 flat surface.
2	It has 5 vertices.	(pyramid)	It has 8 edges.
3	It has 6 flat surfaces.	(cube)	It has 12 edges.
4	It has 0 vertices.	(cylinder)	It has 2 flat surfaces.
5	It has 0 vertices.	(sphere)	It has 0 edges.
6	It has 12 edges.	(rectangular prism)	It has 8 vertices.

To win, be first to cover ten facts on your game board.

Try Again Play again!

Play a Game

Partner Talk

Share your thinking while you work.

Start Get 20 red squares for one player.
Get 20 blue squares for the other player.
Get a . Take turns.

Try Toss the . Count that number of spaces on the game board. Name the picture in each game space. If you see a plane shape, name a solid figure that you can use to trace that plane shape. After you do this, cover the spaces.

Start Here!

Cover the Path!

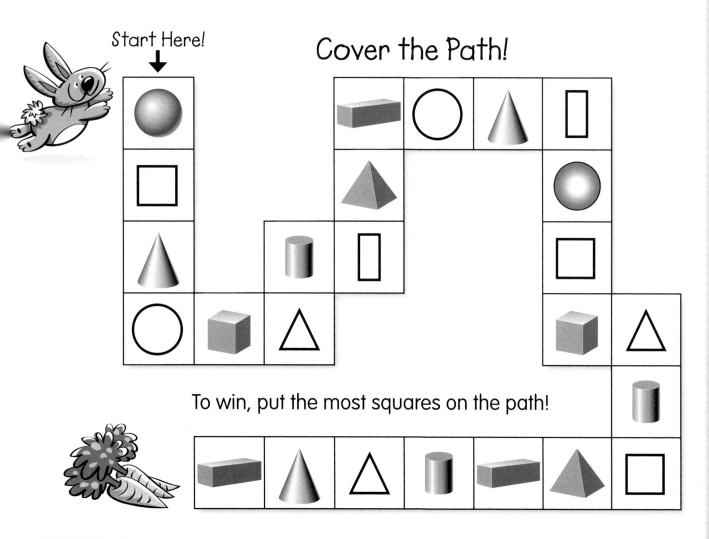

To win, put the most squares on the path!

Try Again Play again!

Play a Game

2 dots	rectangular prism
3 dots	sphere
4 dots	square
5 dots	circle
6 dots	pyramid
7 dots	toss again
8 dots	triangle
9 dots	cylinder
10 dots	cube
11 dots	cone
12 dots	rectangle

Start Get 20 red squares for one player.
Get 20 blue squares for the other player.
Get . Take turns.

Try Toss the . Count the dots.
Read the word next to that number of dots.

IF YOU NAME	COVER
A plane shape	■
A solid figure	■ ■

Start Here!

Cover the Path!

To win, put the most squares on the path!

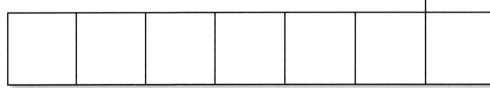

Try Again Play again!

Look and See

Partner Talk

Share your thinking while you work.

Start 🚶 Put 3 4 5 6 7 8 in a 🛍.

Get 8 red squares for Player 1.
Get 8 blue squares for Player 2. Take turns.

Try Pick a tile. Find a shape with that number of vertices.
Place a square on that shape. Lose your turn if the shape is covered.
Put your tile back in the 🛍.

To win, be the first to cover five shapes.

Try Again Remove the squares. Choose a shape. Finger trace smaller
shapes you could use to make the shape you chose.

Look and See

Partner Talk

Share your thinking while you work.

Start Put  2 3 4 in a bag.

Get 8 red squares for Player I.
Get 8 blue squares for Player 2.
Get paper and pencil. Take turns.

Try Pick a tile. Find a picture made by drawing that number of shapes. Place a square on that picture. Lose your turn if there is no picture for you to cover. Put your tile back in the bag.

To win, put the most squares on the game board.

Try Again Draw shapes made with smaller shapes.
Trace these drawings, or make your own drawings.

Center Activity II-3 ★ ★

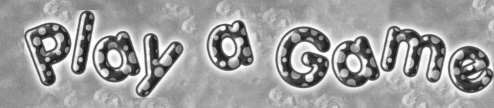

Partner Talk
Share your thinking while you work.

Start Put   in a . Get 18 red squares.

Give one game board to each player. Take turns.

Try Pick a tile.
Find the shape next to that number.
Find a space on your game board with that shape cut into other shapes.
Cover that space.

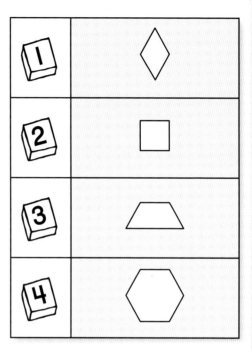

Four Corners

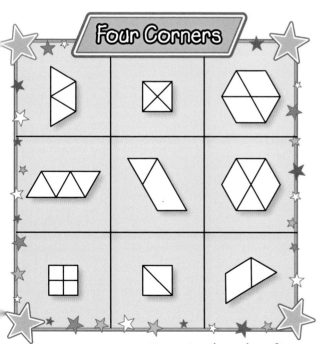

Four Corners

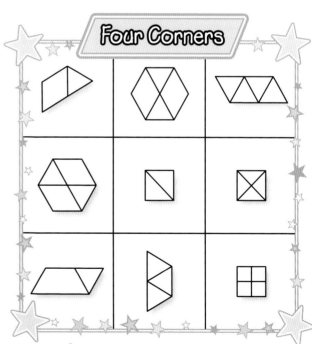

To win, be the first player to cover four corners.

Try Again Play again!

Play a Game

Start Put 1 2 3 4 in a . Get 18 red squares.

Give one game board to each player. Take turns.

Try Pick a tile.
Find the shape next to that number.
Find a space on your game board with that shape cut apart into other shapes. Cover that space.

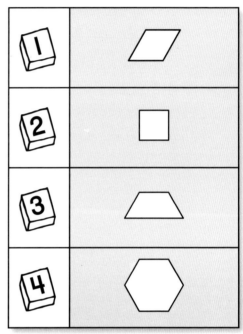

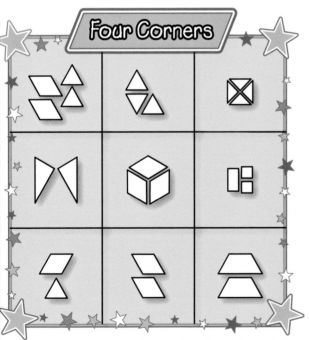

To win, be the first player to cover four corners.

Try Again Play again!

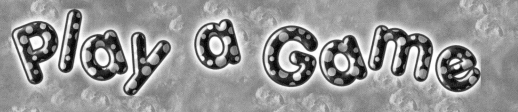

Start 🚶 Get 16 red squares.
Cover each game space with a square.
Take turns.

Try Uncover two game spaces.

If the shapes are congruent, keep the squares.

If not, put the squares back where they were.

Take turns until all the shapes are uncovered.

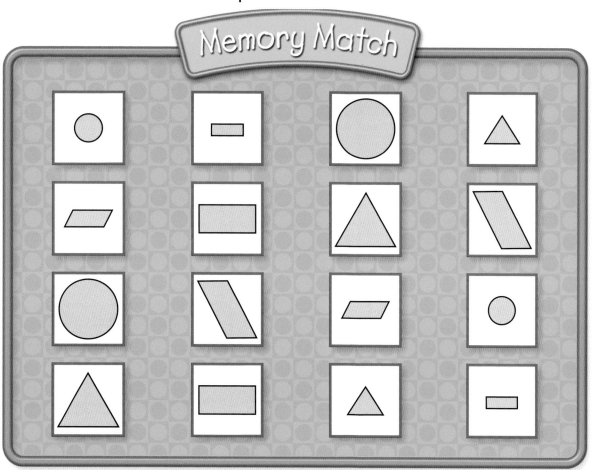

To win, collect the most squares.

Try Again Play again! This time, tell why the two shapes
are congruent, or why they are not congruent.

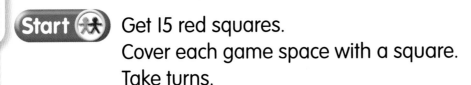

Play a Game

Start 🏃 Get 15 red squares.
Cover each game space with a square.
Take turns.

Try Uncover three game spaces.

If all 3 shapes are congruent, keep the squares.

If not, put the squares back where they were.

Take turns until all the shapes are uncovered.

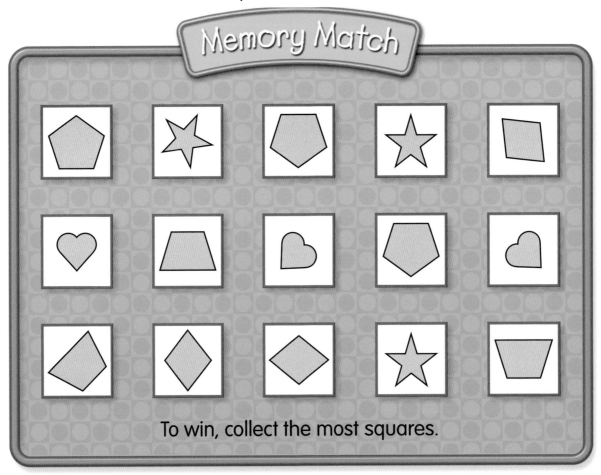

Memory Match

To win, collect the most squares.

Try Again Play again! This time, tell why the three shapes
are congruent, or why they are not congruent.

Center Activity 11-5 ★ ★

Cover Three

Start 👥 Get a 🎲. Get 6 red squares for one player.
Get 6 blue squares for the other player. Take turns.

Try Toss the 🎲. Say the number. Find the shapes next to that number. Tell if the first shape was moved by a translation, a reflection, or a rotation. If you see that word on the game board, cover that word with a square. If not, your turn is over.

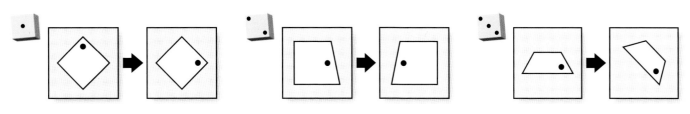

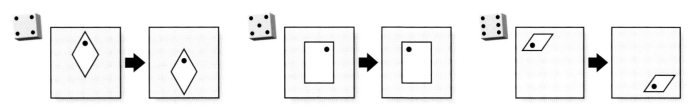

rotation	reflection	translation
reflection	translation	rotation
translation	rotation	reflection

To win, get:

■ ■ ■ or ■ or ■
               ■
               ■
■   or   ■
  ■   ■
   ■ ■

Try Again Play again!

Cover Three

Start 🚶 Put ⬛1 ⬛2 ⬛3 in a 🛍. Get 6 red squares for one player.

Get 6 blue squares for the other player. Take turns.

Try Pick a tile.

If you pick ⬛1, find two shapes that show a translation.

If you pick ⬛2, find two shapes that show a reflection.

If you pick ⬛3, find two shapes that show a rotation.

Use a square to cover the arrow between the shapes.
Put the tile back in the 🛍.

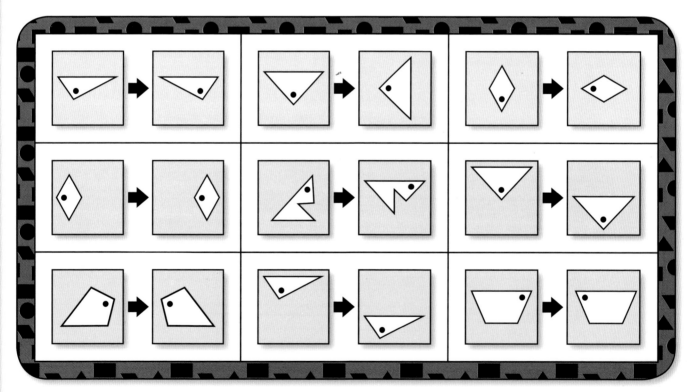

To win, get: ■ ■ ■ or ■ or ■   or   ■

Try Again Play again!

Try Together

Start Put  in a 🛍.

Get 18 red squares. Take turns until the 🛍 is empty.

Try Pick a tile. Take that number of squares. Make part of a shape on the left side of the workmat. Make sure part of the shape touches the line of symmetry. Ask your partner to take the same number of squares. Your partner makes the matching part of your shape on the workmat. Remove the squares.

Line of Symmetry

Try Again Begin again! This time, make some shapes that do not have a line of symmetry.

Try Together

Partner Talk

Share your thinking while you work.

Start 👥 Get 20 red squares. Get a ⬭. Take turns.

Try Look at the bowl of ABC soup. Find a letter that has a line of symmetry. Use the ⬭ to trace its line of symmetry. Cover that letter with a square. Take turns until all letters with a line of symmetry are covered.

Try Again Tell why some of the letters do not have a line of symmetry. Look at the letters in your name. Tell your partner which ones have a line of symmetry.

Look and See

Partner Talk
Share your thinking while you work.

Start Get 6 red squares.
Take turns.

Try Read a riddle. Use the clues to find the figure.
Name that figure. Then use a square to cover it.

Which shape am I?
I have no faces.
I am a solid figure.
I look like something
you bounce.

Which shape am I?
You can roll me.
I have one flat
surface.
I am a solid figure.

Which shape am I?
I have 3 vertices.
I am a plane shape.
I have 3 sides.

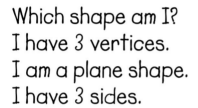

Which shape am I?
I have the same
number of sides as
vertices.
I am a plane shape.
I have 6 sides.

Which shape am I?
I have the same
number of vertices
as sides.
I am a plane shape.
I have 4 sides.

Which shape am I?
I have 2 flat faces.
You can roll me.
I am a solid figure.

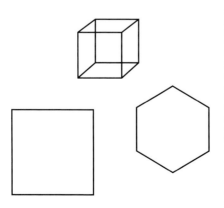

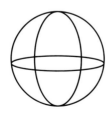

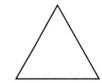

Try Again This time, make up a riddle for each of the remaining figures.

Look and See

Start Get 8 red squares.
Get 1 blue square.
Get 1  .
Work together.

 OR

Try Read a riddle. Use red squares to cover the figures that do not match the clues. Put a blue square below the correct shape. Name that figure. Put a ⬭ below PLANE SHAPE or SOLID FIGURE at the top of the page. Repeat for each riddle.

You can stack me on one end but not the other.
I can be rolled.
Many people enjoy a treat made with this shape.

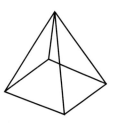

I have 8 sides and 8 vertices.
All my sides are the same length.
I can be used to keep people safe on the road.

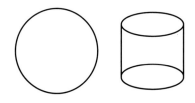

I have 4 sides.
I have 4 vertices.
All my sides are the same length.

I have 6 faces.
You can stack me in any direction.
People like to use me to store many things.

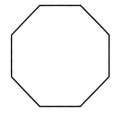

I have no sides and no vertices.
Pizza often comes in my shape.

You can trace triangles on 4 of my faces.
My base is a square.
I have 5 vertices.

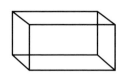

Try Again This time, make up your own riddle for your partner.

Partner Talk

Share your thinking while you work.

Try Together

Start 👫 Put `0` `0` `2` `2` `3` `3` `4` `4` in a 🛍. Take turns.

Try Pick a tile. Place it under a shape with that number of equal parts.

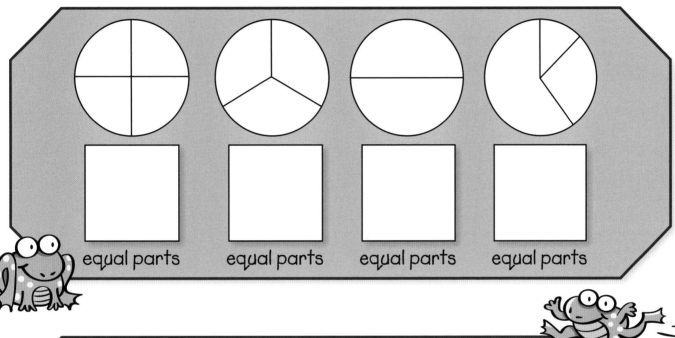

equal parts   equal parts   equal parts   equal parts

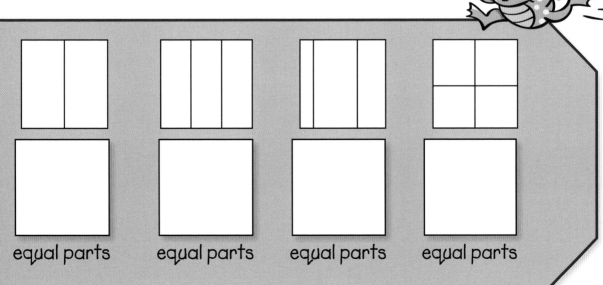

equal parts   equal parts   equal parts   equal parts

Try Again Put the tiles back in the 🛍. Try again. If a shape is split into equal parts, tell if the parts are halves, thirds, or fourths.

Try Together

Partner Talk

Share your thinking while you work.

Start 👫 Put 0 0 2 2 3 3 4 4 in a 🛍. Take turns.

Try Pick a tile. Place it under a shape with that number of equal parts.

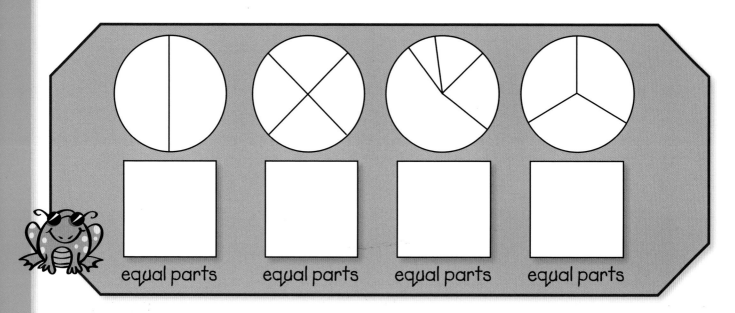

equal parts   equal parts   equal parts   equal parts

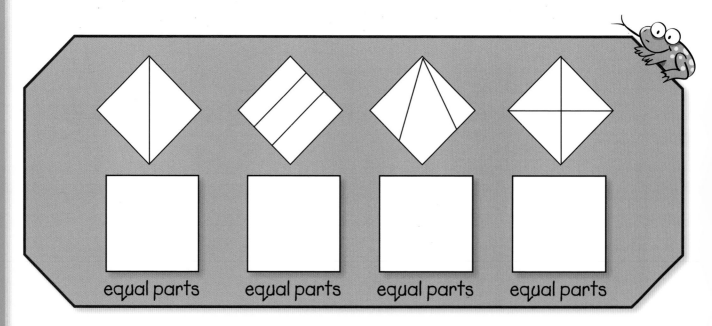

equal parts   equal parts   equal parts   equal parts

Try Again Put the tiles back in the 🛍. Try again. Talk about what you have tried to split into equal parts and why.

Center Activity 12-1 ⭐ ⭐

Math in Motion

Partner Talk
Share your thinking while you work.

 Get   . Take turns.

Try Pick a shape.
Tap on the equal parts as you count them out loud.
Place a ⊂▭ on the fraction for the shaded part of that shape.
Say that fraction out loud.

a 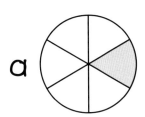 $\dfrac{1}{4}$ $\dfrac{1}{2}$ $\dfrac{1}{5}$ $\dfrac{1}{3}$ $\dfrac{1}{6}$

b 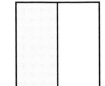 $\dfrac{1}{4}$ $\dfrac{1}{2}$ $\dfrac{1}{5}$ $\dfrac{1}{3}$ $\dfrac{1}{6}$

c 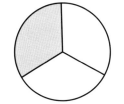 $\dfrac{1}{4}$ $\dfrac{1}{2}$ $\dfrac{1}{5}$ $\dfrac{1}{3}$ $\dfrac{1}{6}$

d $\dfrac{1}{4}$ $\dfrac{1}{2}$ $\dfrac{1}{5}$ $\dfrac{1}{3}$ $\dfrac{1}{6}$

e 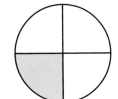 $\dfrac{1}{4}$ $\dfrac{1}{2}$ $\dfrac{1}{5}$ $\dfrac{1}{3}$ $\dfrac{1}{6}$

Try Again Remove the ⊂▭ . Try again.
Trace each shape and its equal parts in the air.

Math in Motion

Start Get  . Take turns.

Try Pick a shape. Tap on the equal parts as you count them out loud. Place a on the fraction for the white part of that shape. Say that fraction out loud.

a.  $\dfrac{3}{4}$ $\dfrac{3}{2}$ $\dfrac{3}{5}$ $\dfrac{3}{3}$ $\dfrac{3}{6}$

b. $\dfrac{2}{4}$ $\dfrac{2}{2}$ $\dfrac{2}{5}$ $\dfrac{2}{3}$ $\dfrac{2}{6}$

c. 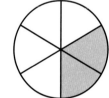 $\dfrac{4}{4}$ $\dfrac{4}{2}$ $\dfrac{4}{5}$ $\dfrac{4}{3}$ $\dfrac{4}{6}$

d. 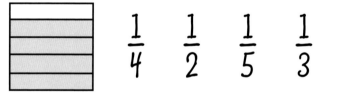 $\dfrac{1}{4}$ $\dfrac{1}{2}$ $\dfrac{1}{5}$ $\dfrac{1}{3}$ $\dfrac{1}{6}$

e. 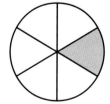 $\dfrac{5}{4}$ $\dfrac{5}{2}$ $\dfrac{5}{5}$ $\dfrac{5}{6}$ $\dfrac{5}{3}$

Try Again Remove the . Try again. Talk about when a teacher might want to split something into equal parts.

Start 🚶 Get 12 red squares.

Cover each game space with a square. Take turns.

Try Uncover two game spaces.

If you see a circle and a fraction for the shaded part of that circle, keep the squares.

If not, put the squares back where they were.

Take turns until all the spaces are uncovered.

Memory Match

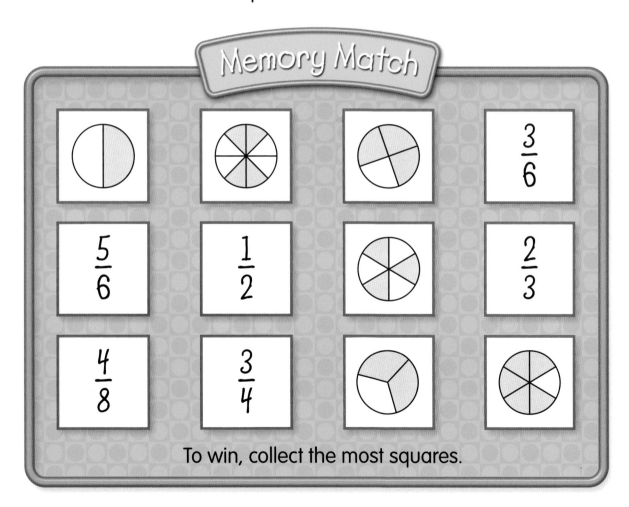

To win, collect the most squares.

Try Again Play again!

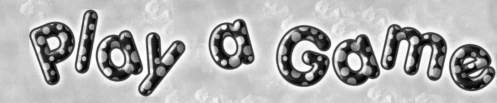

Start 🚶 Get .

Get 9 red squares.

Cover each game space with a square. Take turns.

Try Toss the 🎲. Say the fraction next to your dots. Uncover a game space. Do you have the fraction for the shaded part of the shape?

If **YES**, keep the square.

If **NO**, put the square back where it was.

Take turns until one player wins.

Memory Match

To win, collect 5 squares.

⚀	$\frac{3}{5}$
⚁	$\frac{5}{6}$
⚂	$\frac{2}{3}$
⚃	$\frac{3}{4}$
⚄	$\frac{5}{8}$
⚅	$\frac{1}{2}$

Try Again Play again!

Center Activity 12-3 ⭐ ⭐

Look and See

Partner Talk
Share your thinking while you work.

Start Get  . Take turns.

Try Decide how much of the spider's web you see. Choose 1, 2, or 3. Place a ⟨paperclip⟩ on your choice.

A.

Is this spider
1. just starting her web?
2. almost finished?
3. half done with her web?

B.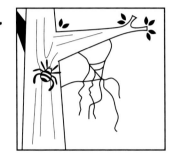

The spider returned to find her web was:
1. almost gone.
2. $\frac{1}{2}$ gone.
3. in good shape.

C.

"Now," she says,
1. "I'm half done."
2. "I have just started."
3. "I am almost finished."

D.

This time she finds her web
1. $\frac{1}{2}$ gone.
2. almost gone.
3. all there.

Try Again Draw a spider web that is just started, or about half done, or almost finished.

Look and See

Partner Talk

Share your thinking while you work.

Start 🏃 Get 🎲.
Get 25 squares.
Take turns.

Try Toss the 🎲. Read the description next to that number.
Use squares to cover about that much of the floor.

⚀	About $\frac{1}{2}$ done
⚁	About 1 whole floor done
⚂	About 0 done
⚃	About $\frac{1}{2}$ done
⚄	About 1 whole floor done
⚅	About 0 done

TILES TILES

Try Again Remove the squares. Repeat until each player gets 3 turns.
Talk about how covering a floor with squares is like putting
pieces in a puzzle.

Try Together

Partner Talk

Share your thinking while you work.

Start 👫 Get 6 red squares.
Take turns until all the fractions are covered.

Try Point to a fishbowl. Tell how many fish are striped.
Ask your partner to tell how many fish are in the set.
Look at the fractions below the fishbowls.
Cover the fraction that shows the striped part of the set.

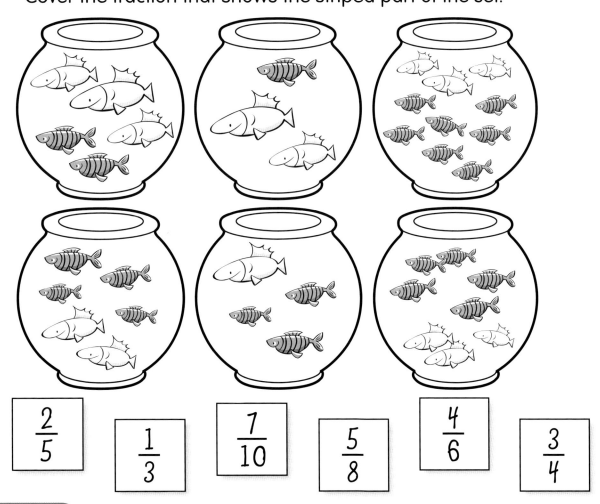

$$\frac{2}{5}$$ $$\frac{1}{3}$$ $$\frac{7}{10}$$ $$\frac{5}{8}$$ $$\frac{4}{6}$$ $$\frac{3}{4}$$

Try Again Make sure that all the fractions are covered.
Point to a fishbowl. Then uncover a fraction.
If the fraction shows the part of the group with striped fish,
keep the square. If not, put the square back where it was.
Take turns until every fraction is uncovered.

Try Together

Share your thinking while you work.

Start 🏃 Get ⓪ ① ② ③ ④ ⑤ ⑥ ⑦ ⑧ ⑨ .

Take turns until each partner gets 5 or more turns.

Try Point to a fishbowl. Ask your partner about part of the set of fish.
For example, ask: *What part of the set is striped?*
Or ask: *What part of the set is not striped?*
Show your partner's answer below with number tiles.

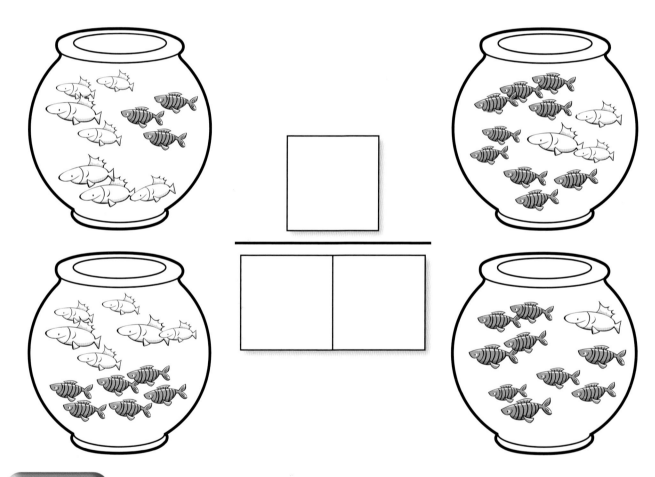

Try Again This time, choose a fishbowl. Do not tell your partner which one. Make a fraction with tiles. Show what part of the set of fish is swimming at the top of the fishbowl, or at the bottom of the fishbowl. Ask your partner to say your fraction and point to the fish in your fishbowl.

Center Activity 12-5 ★ ★

 **Try Together**

Partner Talk
Share your thinking while you work.

 **Start** Get 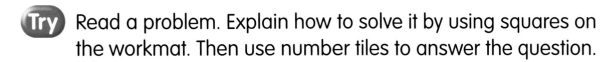 1 2 3 4 5 6 7 8 9 .

Get 20 red squares. Work together.

Try Read a problem. Explain how to solve it by using squares on the workmat. Then use number tiles to answer the question.

a. A store has 20 cans of vegetables on a shelf. $\frac{3}{4}$ of the cans contain corn. How many cans of corn are on the shelf?

CORN
CORN

b. Steve has 15 toy cars. $\frac{1}{5}$ of them are blue. How many cars are blue?

c. Peg is working on a puzzle that has 18 pieces. She has $\frac{2}{3}$ of the pieces in place. How many more pieces will complete the puzzle?

 **WORKMAT**

Try Again Make up a problem that has a fraction. Ask a partner to solve your problem.

Try Together

Partner Talk

Share your thinking while you work.

Start 🐞 Get  1 2 3 4 5 6 7 8 9 .

Get 24 squares.

Get a ⬭ . Work together.

Try Pick a star with a fraction. Put a ⬭ under it.
Choose a problem. Read the problem with the fraction you chose.
Explain how to solve the problem with squares on the workmat.
Show your answer with tiles.

a. Karen has a stamp collection. On one page, there are 24 stamps. _____ of them are flag stamps. How many flag stamps are on that page?

b. The librarian added 12 new books to the library. _____ of them are science books. How many new science books did the librarian add?

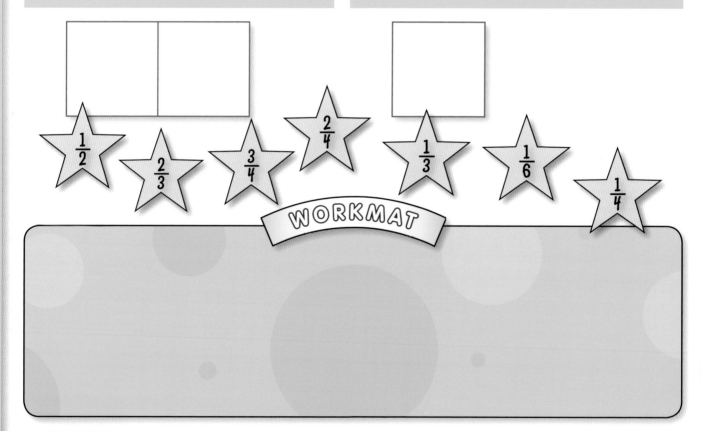

WORKMAT

Try Again Solve the first problem again with $\frac{1}{8}$, $\frac{3}{8}$, $\frac{5}{8}$, or $\frac{7}{8}$.

Look and See

Start 👥 Get  .

Get 4 red squares. Get 4 blue squares. Work together.

Try Point to an object. Name it.

Say an attribute you can measure for that object.

Tell which tool you would use to measure that attribute.

Cover the object with a red square if you can measure its capacity, a blue square if you can measure its weight, and a ⬭ if you can measure its length. Choose one attribute for each object.

Try Again Tell some ways that you measure at home.

Center Activity 13-1 ⭐

Look and See

Partner Talk

Share your thinking while you work.

Start 👫 Get 9 red squares. Work together.

Try Choose an object. Name it.
Talk about two attributes you can measure for that object.
Talk about which tool you could use to measure each attribute.
Cover the object with a square.

Length

ATTRIBUTES

Weight

Capacity

Try Again Tell some ways that you measure at home.

Helping Hands

Start 👥 Get 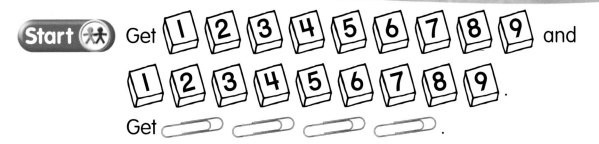 and

. Get ⬯ ⬯ ⬯ ⬯ .

Try Work together. Choose an object. How many ⬯ do you think it will take to measure its length? Use a tile to show your estimate. Place ⬯ end-to-end to measure.

Estimate

Measurement

Try Again Estimate and measure the length of the bottom of this page.

Helping Hands

Partner Talk
Share your thinking while you work.

Start  or Get 1 2 3 4 5 6 7 8 9 and
1 2 3 4 5 6 7 8 9 .

Get ⬭ ⬭ ⬭ ⬭ . Get 10 red squares.

Try Work together. Choose an object.
How many ⬭ do you think it will take to measure its length.
Use a tile to show your estimate.
Place ⬭ end-to-end to measure.
Use a tile to show your measurement.

Estimate

Measurement

Try Again Estimate and measure each object again using squares.
Tell what happens and why.

Listen and Learn

Share your thinking while you work.

Start 🚶 Get  .

Try Point to an object. Measure it with your thumb. Ask your partner to measure it with a ⬭ .

How do the size of your thumb and the size of the ⬭ affect the measurement?

Try Again Count the number of thumbs or ⬭ you need to measure across the bottom of this page.

Center Activity 13-3 ★

Listen and Learn

Start 👤 Get  and

Get ⬭ ⬭ ⬭ ⬭ . Get 10 red squares.

Try Choose an object. Measure it with your thumb. Use a number tile to record the measurement. Next, use a ⬭ and then squares to measure the same object. Why are the results different?

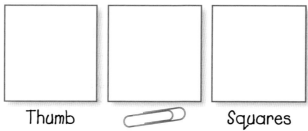

Thumb ⬭ Squares

Try Again Measure a pencil or a crayon in three ways.

Cover Three

Partner Talk
Share your thinking while you work.

Start 👥 Get 6 red squares for one player.
Get 6 blue squares for the other player.
Get 10 red squares. Use these to cover the objects.
Take turns.

Try Uncover an object.
Tell if its length would be about one inch, one foot, or one yard.
If you see that length on the game board, cover it with a square.

1 inch	1 yard	1 foot
1 foot	1 inch	1 yard
1 yard	1 foot	1 inch

To win, get: ■ ■ ■ or ■ or ■ or

Try Again Play again!

Cover Three

Partner Talk

Share your thinking while you work.

Start 👤 Get 6 red squares for one player.
Get 6 blue squares for the other player.
Get 10 red squares. Use these to cover the objects.
Take turns.

36 inches = 1 yard

12 inches = 1 foot

Try Uncover a word. Read the word. Tell if the length of the object would be about one inch, one foot, or one yard.
If you see that length on the game board, cover it with a square.

| bunny | | vase | | beetle | | celery | doll |

spider

stamp

window

| baseball bat | | | | | | | desk |

1 inch	1 yard	1 foot
12 inches	36 inches	1 inch
1 foot	1 inch	36 inches

To win, get: ■ ■ ■ or ■ or ■ or ■

Try Again Play again!

Try Together

Partner Talk

Share your thinking while you work.

Start 👫 Get 5 red squares. Work together.

Try Read a question. Look at the object.
Decide if you would measure it in centimeters or meters.
Put a square below your answer. Point to your choice.

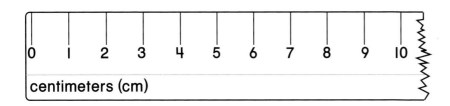

100 centimeters = 1 meter (m)

How would you measure the height of a door?
cm   m

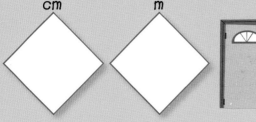

How would you measure the length of a fence?
cm   m

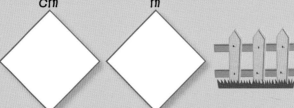

How would you measure the length of a carrot?
cm   m

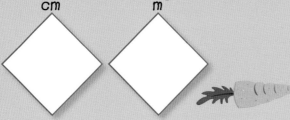

How would you measure the length of a stamp?
cm   m

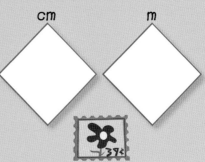

How would you measure the length of a ladybug?
cm   m

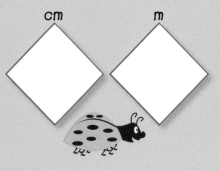

Try Again This time, estimate the length of each object.
Tell what you think it would be.

Try Together

Start Get ⌐⌐ ⌐⌐ ⌐⌐ ⌐⌐ . Work together.

Try Read a question. Explain why each possible answer is or is not the correct answer to the question. Place a ⌐⌐ below the correct answer.

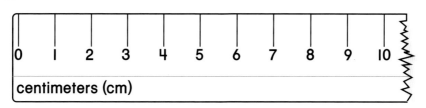

centimeters (cm)

Which piece of fruit is about one centimeter long?

| apple | cherry | orange | blueberry |

Which object is about one meter long?

| book | window | cookie | pen |

Which vegetable is about one centimeter long?

| carrot | pea | tomato | celery |

Which toy is about a meter long?

| Fire truck | car | doll | ball |

Try Again This time, estimate the length of each object named on this page. Tell what you think it would be.

Center Activity 13-5 ⭐ ⭐

Helping Hands

Start 🚶 Get 7 red squares. Work together.

Try Carl the Carpenter makes many things in his workshop.
Pick an item and find its perimeter. Use a square to cover the answer.
Continue until every answer is covered.

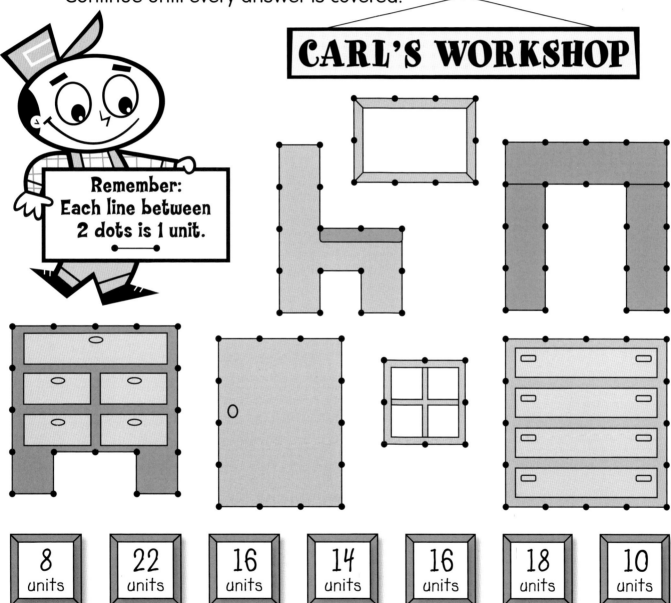

Remember:
Each line between
2 dots is 1 unit.

CARL'S WORKSHOP

| 8 units | 22 units | 16 units | 14 units | 16 units | 18 units | 10 units |

Try Again Begin again! This time, say the items in order
from least perimeter to greatest perimeter.

Helping Hands

Start  Put 20 red squares in a . Take turns.

Try Take some squares from the 🛍️. Make a shape on the workmat by using all of the squares. Ask your partner to find the perimeter of your shape. Say its perimeter.
Then put the squares back in the 🛍️.

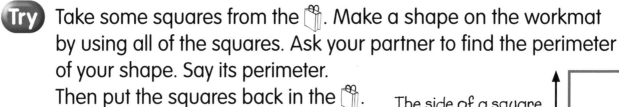
The side of a square is one unit.

Say: "The perimeter is _____ units."
Take turns until each player gets five turns.

Try Again This time, try to make animal shapes with your squares.

Look and See

Partner Talk

Share your thinking while you work.

Start 👫 Get ③ ④ ⑤ ⑥ ⑦ ⑧ ⑨.

Get 10 red squares. Work together.

Try Point to a shape. Use squares to find its area.
Count the square units inside that shape.
Use a number tile to show the area of the shape.

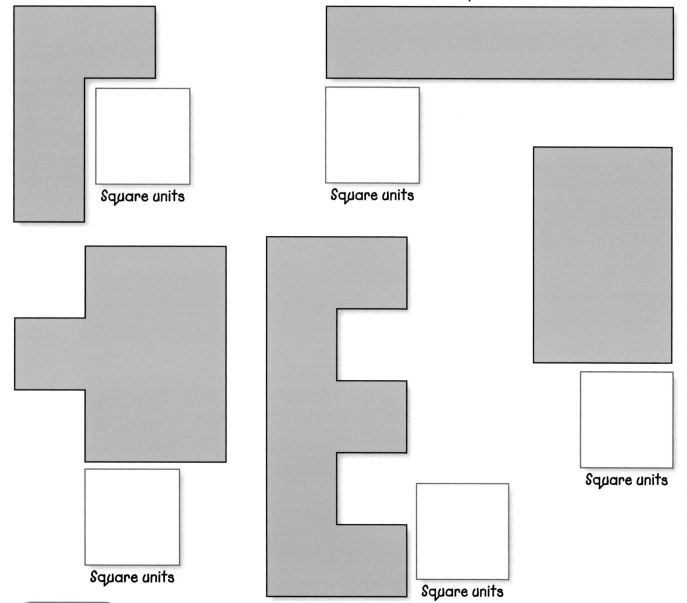

Square units

Square units

Square units

Square units

Square units

Try Again This time, pick a tile.
Make your own shape with that number of square units.

Look and See

Partner Talk

Share your thinking while you work.

Start 👥 Get  .

Get 10 red squares. Work together.

Try Choose a shape. Estimate the number of square units in that shape. Use squares to find the area.
Use a number tile to show the area of the shape.

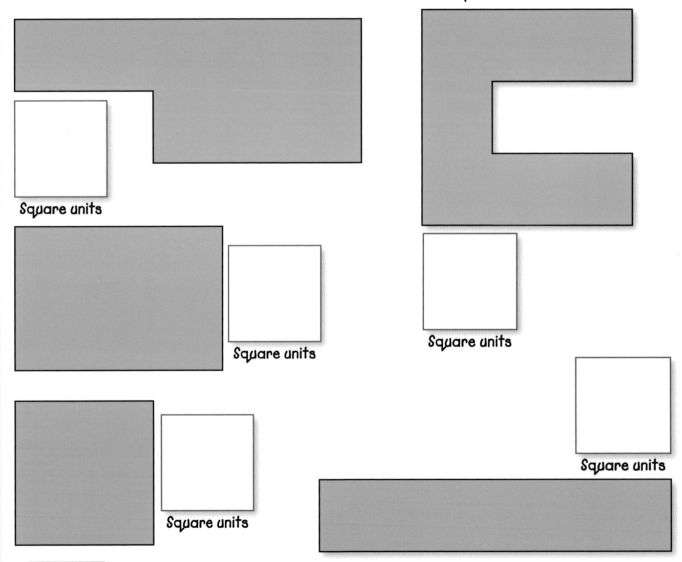

Square units

Square units

Square units

Square units

Square units

Square units

Try Again Talk about objects in your classroom that you can measure with the red squares.
Estimate the area of each of those objects.

Center Activity 13-7 ⭐ ⭐

Look and See

Start  Get 3 red squares. Get 15 blue squares.
Work together.

Try Teddy Bear goes for a walk. Along the way, he wants to know the area of each friend's yard. Use blue squares to make each yard. Tell Teddy Bear the area of each one.

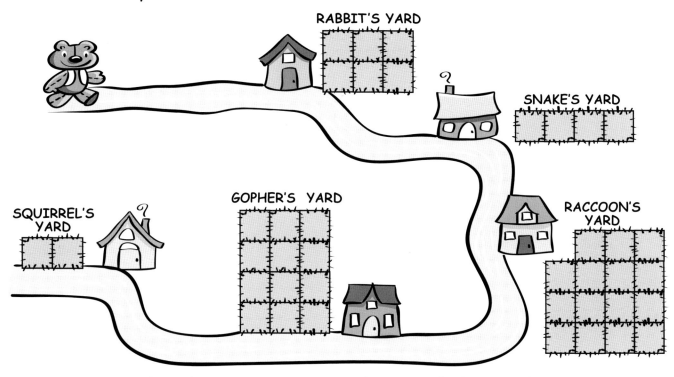

RABBIT'S YARD

SNAKE'S YARD

GOPHER'S YARD

SQUIRREL'S YARD

RACCOON'S YARD

Now read each question. Put a red square below each answer.

1. What is the area of the Gopher's yard?		2. Which animal's yard has an area of 6 square units?		3. Whose yard has the greatest area?	
10 square units	12 square units	Rabbit's yard	Snake's yard	Raccoon's yard	Gopher's yard

Try Again  Make a yard for a different animal.
Ask your partner to find its area.

Look and See

Partner Talk
Share your thinking while you work.

Start 🏃 Get I red square to answer the question.

Get [0] [1] [2] [3] [4] [5] [6] [7] [8] [9]

and [0] [1] [2] [3] [4] [5] [6] [7] [8] [9].

Get 16 blue squares. Work together.

Try Use blue squares to show each animal's habitat. Use number tiles to record the area. Then find the distance around each habitat. Use number tiles to record it.

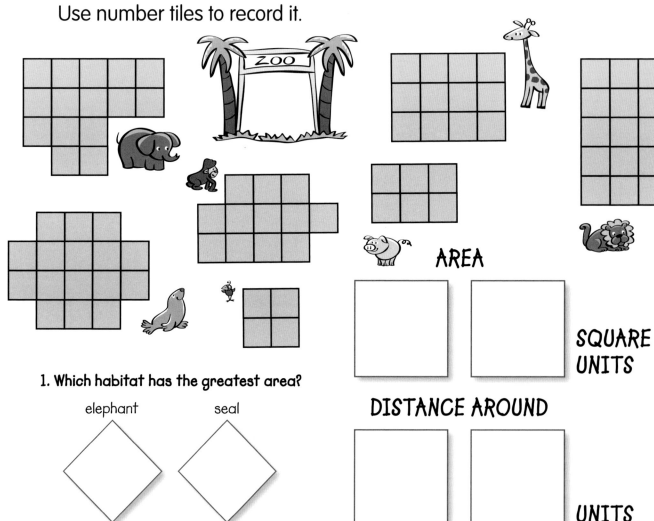

AREA

SQUARE UNITS

1. Which habitat has the greatest area?

elephant   seal

DISTANCE AROUND

UNITS

Try Again Which animals have the least space?
Which animals have the most space?

Try Together

Partner Talk

Share your thinking while you work.

Start 👫 Put  in a 🛍 .

Get 10 red squares for one player.
Get 10 blue squares for the other player.
Work together. Name each container.
Tell if it holds more or less than the container of milk.

Try Pick a title. If you choose ⬜0 , place a square on a container

that holds less than the container of milk, if you see one.

If you choose ⬜1 , place a square on a container that

holds more than the container of milk, if you see one. Put your

tile back in the 🛍 . Take turns until every picture is covered.

Try Again Remove your squares. Play again!

Try Together

Start 🚶 Get .
Get ⬭ ⬭.
Take turns until each partner gets 5 or more turns.

Try Toss the 🎲 🎲. Say the number of dots in all.
Put a ⬭ below the picture with that number.
Toss the 🎲 🎲 again. Say the number of dots in all.
Put a ⬭ below the picture with that number.
Ask your partner to tell you if the capacity of the first container
is more than, less than, or the same as the capacity of the second.

Try Again Work together. Name these containers in order
from greatest to least capacity.

Look and See

Partner Talk
Share your thinking while you work.

Start 🏃 Put   in a 🛍.

Take turns.

Try Pick a tile.
Look at the picture next to that tile number.
Find the picture of a container on the right that
would hold about the same amount.
Cover that picture with your tile.

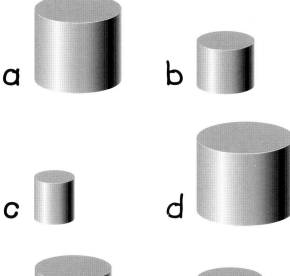

Try Again Remove the tiles. Take turns. Point to a container on the right.
Ask your partner to point to the containers on the left that
would hold about the same amount.

Look and See

Partner Talk

Share your thinking while you work.

Start Get   .

Take turns.

Try Point to a jar of marbles. To get the number of marbles in the jar, about how many times would you fill this small container? Display a number tile to show your estimate.

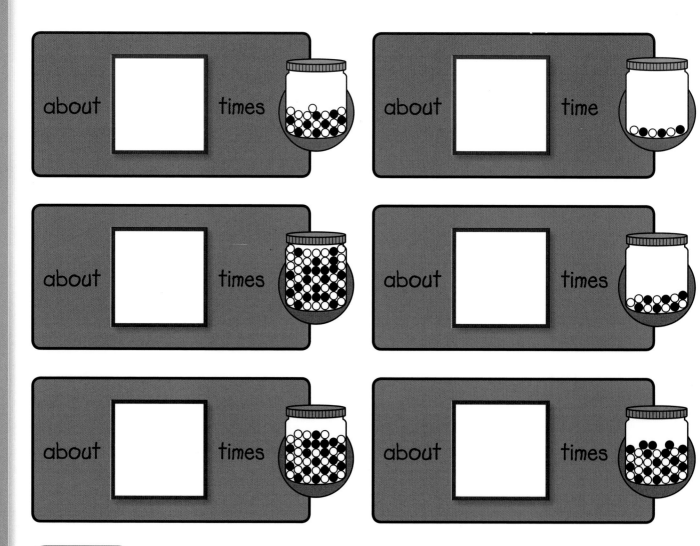

about ___ times

about ___ time

about ___ times

about ___ times

about ___ times

about ___ times

Try Again Remove the tiles. Talk about other small containers that you can use to fill a larger container. For example, you can fill a cup and empty it into a bowl.

 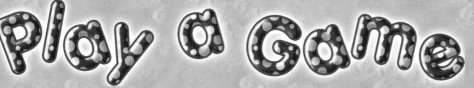

Start 🚶 Get 12 red squares. Cover each game space with a square. Take turns.

Try Uncover two game spaces.
Do you see a picture of a container,
and the amount that the container holds?

  If you do, name the container, say its capacity,
  and then keep the squares.

  If you do not, put the squares back where they were.

Take turns until all the spaces are uncovered.

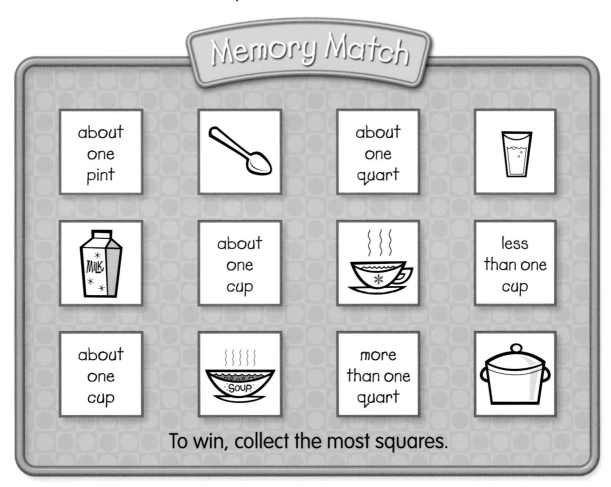

Memory Match

about one pint	🥄	about one quart	🥛
🥛MILK	about one cup	☕	less than one cup
about one cup	🍲SOUP	more than one quart	🍯

To win, collect the most squares.

Try Again Play again!

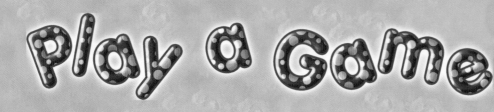

Partner
Talk

Share your thinking while you work.

Start 👫 Get 12 red squares.
Cover each game space with a square. Take turns.

Try Uncover three game spaces.
Do you see a capacity, and two pictures of containers that have about that capacity?

If you do, name the containers, say their capacity, and then keep the squares.

If you do not, put the squares back where they were.

Take turns until all the spaces are uncovered.

Memory Match

about one pint		about one quart	
	about one cup		
			more than one quart

To win, collect the most squares.

Try Again Play again!

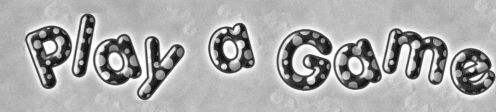

Partner Talk
Share your thinking while you work.

Start 🚶 Get a 🎲. Get 20 blue squares.
Get one red square and one ⫘ for game markers.
Give one game marker to each player. Take turns.

Try Toss the 🎲. Move your marker that number of spaces.
Name the container in the space where you land. If that container's capacity is about the same as or less than a liter, explain why. Collect one blue square. If not, stay on your game space but do not collect a square. Play until both players reach the finish line.

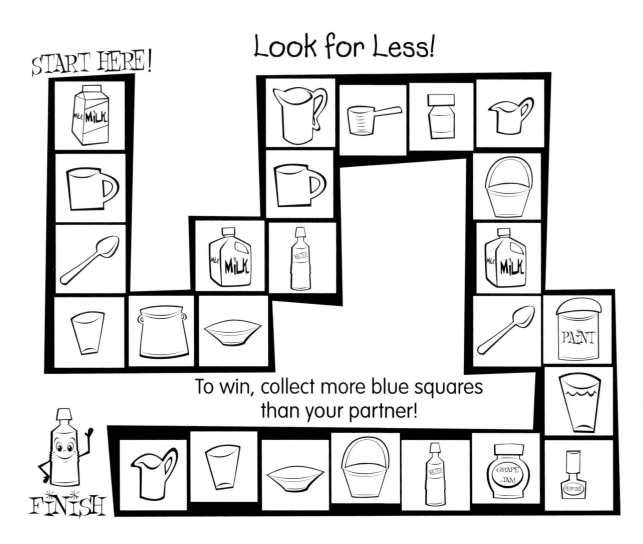

START HERE!

Look for Less!

To win, collect more blue squares than your partner!

FINISH

Try Again Play again!

Play a Game

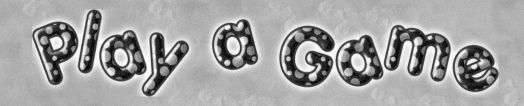

Start 🚶 Get a 🎲. Get 20 blue squares.
Get one red square and one ⬭ for game markers.
Give one game marker to each player. Take turns.

Try Toss the 🎲. Move your marker that number of spaces. Name the container in the space where you land. If that container's capacity is about the same as or more than a liter, explain why. Then collect one blue square. If not, stay on your game space but do not collect a square. Play until both players reach the finish line.

Measure More!

START HERE!

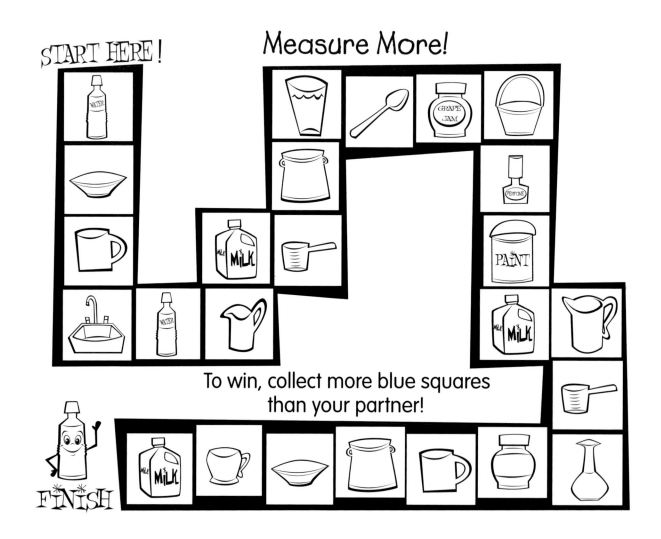

To win, collect more blue squares than your partner!

FINISH

Try Again Play again!

Listen and Learn

Partner Talk

Share your thinking while you work.

Start   Get 🎲 🎲.
Get 12 red squares. Get 12 blue squares.
Decide which colored bag each player will use
on a scale. Take turns.

Try Each player tosses 🎲 🎲 and takes that number
of squares. Pretend your squares are boxes of raisins.
Whose boxes are heavier?

Choose a scale. Put your boxes in your bag.
Your partner puts the other boxes in the other bag.

Tell how you know that the boxes are
on the correct scale.

Try Again Remove your squares. Begin again!

Listen and Learn

Partner Talk
Share your thinking while you work.

Start Get 🎲 🎲. Get 12 red squares. Get 12 blue squares.

Get
0 1 1 2 3 4 5 6 7 8 9 .

Decide which colored bag each player
will use on the scale. Take turns.

Try Each player tosses 🎲 🎲 and takes that number of squares.
Pretend your squares are boxes of raisins. Whose boxes are lighter?

Choose a scale. Put your boxes in your bag.
Your partner puts the other boxes in the other bag.

Tell how you know that the boxes are on the correct scale.
Then use tiles to answer the question.

Question

?

If you want both bags to
have the same weight, how
many boxes of raisins should
you add to one bag?

Display your answer here.

Try Again Remove your squares and tiles. Begin again!

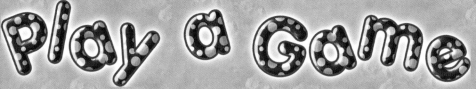

Start 👥 Put 🔲 🔳 in a 🛍️ . Get 18 red squares.

Give one game board to each player. Take turns.

Try Pick a tile. If you pick 🔲 , find something that you would measure in ounces. Cover it with a square. If you pick 🔳 , find something that you would measure in pounds. Cover it with a square. Lose your turn if you cannot find a space to cover. Put the tile back in the 🛍️.

> **Hint:**
> Lighter items are measured in ounces.
> Heavier items are measured in pounds.

Cover Nine

chair	checker	refrigerator
sticker	desk	marker
crayon	encyclopedia	paper clip

Cover Nine

dictionary	eraser	bag of potatoes
piano bench	safety pin	glue stick
pencil	pencil sharpener	marble

To win, be the first player to cover nine game spaces.

Try Again Play again!

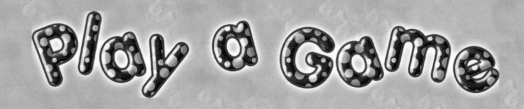

Partner Talk

Share your thinking while you work.

Start  Get ⬚1 ⬚2 ⬚3 ⬚4 ⬚5 ⬚6 ⬚7 ⬚8 ⬚9 .

Get 18 red squares. Get a 🎲 .
Give one game board to each player. Take turns.

Try Toss the 🎲 . If the number is even, cover an item that you would measure in pounds. If the number is odd, cover an item that you would measure in ounces.

> **Hint:**
> Lighter items are measured in ounces.
> Heavier items are measured in pounds.

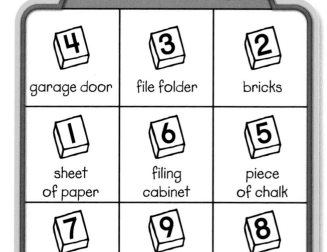

Cover Nine

⬚4	⬚3	⬚2
piano	table	marker
⬚1	⬚6	⬚5
checker	bookshelf	number cube
⬚7	⬚9	⬚8
pen	backpack	feather

Cover Nine

⬚4	⬚3	⬚2
garage door	file folder	bricks
⬚1	⬚6	⬚5
sheet of paper	filing cabinet	piece of chalk
⬚7	⬚9	⬚8
number tile	bag of groceries	television

To win, be the first player to cover nine game spaces.

Try Again Choose a game board. Use your tiles to order the items in that game board from lightest to heaviest. Line up your tiles along the bottom edge of this activity sheet. Repeat with the items on the other game board.

Cover Three

Start  Put ⟦0⟧ ⟦1⟧ in a 🛍️.

Get 6 red squares.
Get 6 blue squares.
Take turns.

Hint:
Lighter items are measured in grams.

Heavier items are measured in kilograms.

Try Pick a tile. If you pick ⟦0⟧, find something that you would measure in grams. Cover it with a square. If you pick ⟦1⟧, find something that you would measure in kilograms. Cover it with a square. Lose your turn if you cannot find a picture to cover. Put the tile back in the 🛍️.

To win, get: ■■■ or ■ or ■ or ■

Try Again Play again!

Cover Three

Partner Talk

Share your thinking while you work.

Start 👫 Get a 🎲.
Get 6 red squares.
Get 6 blue squares.
Take turns.

Hint:
Lighter items are measured in grams.

Heavier items are measured in kilograms.

Try Toss the 🎲. If your number is even, find something that you would measure in grams. Cover it with a square. If your number is odd, find something that you would measure in kilograms. Cover it with a square. Lose your turn if you cannot find a space to cover.

feather	piano	glue stick
computer	quarter	box of crayons
sheet of paper	notebook	bicycle

To win, get: ■ ■ ■ or ■ or ■   or

Try Again Play again!

  Play a Game

Start Get . Put 1 2 3 in a .

Get 20 red squares. Take turns.

Try Toss the . Say the number of dots in all. Name the object next to that number. Pick a tile from the 🛍. Read the question next to that tile number. If your answer is "yes," explain how you would measure. Collect one square. If your answer is "no," your turn is over. Put the tile back in the 🛍.

2

3

4

Question
?

1 Can you measure its length?

2 Can you measure its capacity?

3 Can you measure its weight?

5

6

7

8

9   10   11

12

To win, be the first player to collect 10 squares!

Try Again Play again!

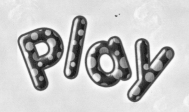

Share your thinking while you work.

Start Get 20 red squares. Get 7 blue squares.

Get [dice]. Take turns.

Try Toss the [dice]. Add the dots. If the object next to that number is already covered, lose your turn. If not, name that object. Then answer every question. Collect a red square every time your answer is "yes." When you finish, cover the picture with a blue square. Play until 7 objects are covered.

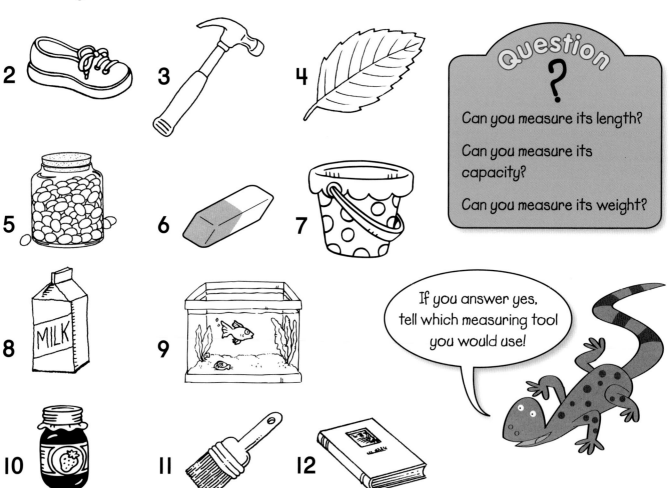

Question

?

Can you measure its length?

Can you measure its capacity?

Can you measure its weight?

If you answer yes, tell which measuring tool you would use!

2 3 4

5 6 7

8 9

10 11 12

The player who collects the most squares wins!

Try Again Play again!

Helping Hands

Start  Get ⓪ ⓪ ① ① ② ② ③ ③ ④ ④ ⑤ ⑤ ⑥ ⑦ ⑧ ⑨ . Get one large 🖇 and one small 🖇 . Take turns.

Try Use tiles. Show a time on the digital clock with 5, 10, 15, 20, 25, 30, 35, 40, 45, 50, or 55 minutes after an hour. Ask your partner to show the same time on the round clock with 🖇 and 🖇 . Say that time. Repeat until each partner gets 6 turns.

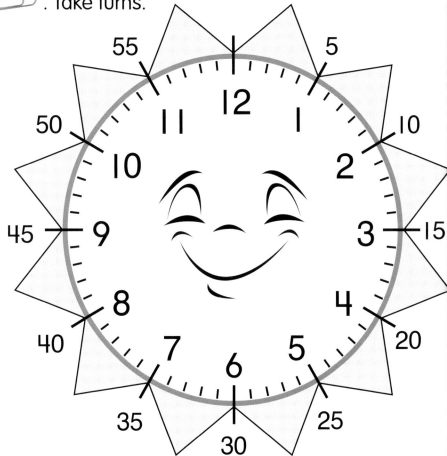

Try Again This time, show a time on the round clock. Ask your partner to show that time on the digital clock.

Helping Hands

Share your thinking while you work.

Start 👫 Get 0 0 1 1 2 2 3 3 4 4 5 5 6 7 8 9 . Get one large ⊂⊃ and one small ⊂⊃ . Take turns.

Try Use tiles. Show a time on the digital clock with 5, 10, 15, 20, 25, 30, 35, 40, 45, 50, or 55 minutes after an hour. Ask your partner to show one hour later than that time on the round clock with ⊂⊃ and ⊂⊃ . Say both times. Repeat until each partner gets 6 turns.

Try Again This time, show one hour earlier than the time on the digital clock.

Try Together

Start 👫 Put **6 7 8 9** in a 🛍.

Get **0 1 2 3 4 5 6 7 8 9**

and **1 2 3 4 5**.

Get a 🎲. Take turns.

Try Pick a tile. Place it in the space next to the table. Toss the 🎲.
Ask your partner to say a time using the words next to the
toss and the number you chose. Put tiles on the clock to show
that time. Repeat until each player gets 6 turns.

⚀	Quarter past
⚁	Half past
⚂	Quarter to
⚃	20 minutes after
⚄	15 minutes before
⚅	15 minutes after

Put your tile here.

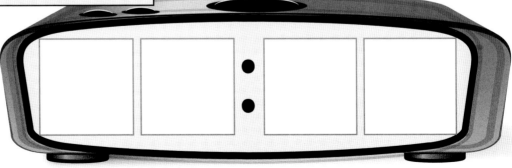

Try Again Play again! Tell what you are doing during the day
at each time that you show on the clock.

Try Together

Partner Talk
Share your thinking while you work.

Start 👫 Put 6 7 8 9 in a 🛍.

Get 0 1 2 3 4 5 6 7 8 9

and 0 1 2 3 4 5 .

Get a 🎲. Take turns.

Try Pick a tile. Place it in the space next to the table. Toss the 🎲.
Ask your partner to say a time using the words next to the
toss and the number you chose. Put tiles on the clock. Show the time
that is one hour later. Repeat until each player gets 6 turns.

⚀	25 minutes after
⚁	Quarter past
⚂	10 minutes before
⚃	Half past
⚄	45 minutes after
⚅	Quarter to

Put your tile here.

Try Again Play again! Tell what you are doing during the day
at each time that you show on the clock.

 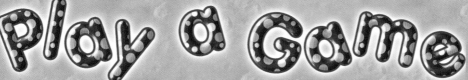

Share your thinking while you work.

 Put ① ② ③ ④ in a 🛍.

Get 10 red squares for one player.
Get 10 blue squares for the other player.
Take turns.

 Seconds

 Minutes

 Hours

 Days

Try Pick a tile. Say the word next to that tile number.
Find an activity you can do in that amount of time.
Use a square to cover your choice.
Lose your turn if you cannot find an activity to cover.
Put the tile back in the 🛍.

go on vacation	snap your fingers ten times	say "Happy Birthday"	say the months of the year	practice the piano
put on a shoe	take a walk	give your teacher a compliment	clean the house	read a chapter book	go to a movie
kick a goal	write your name	go to camp	go out to eat	sing a song

To win, have the most squares on the game board
after every activity is covered.

Try Again Play again! Or think of other activities.
Play the game using your activities.

Center Activity 15-3 ⭐   Topic 15   **5**

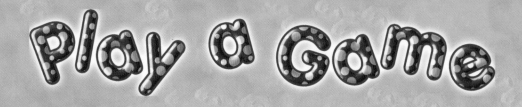

Partner Talk

Share your thinking while you work.

Start 👥 Get 12 red squares. Cover each game space with a square. Take turns.

Try Point to an estimated time. Uncover one game space.
If you can do the activity in that amount of time, keep the square.
If not, put the square back where it was.
Take turns until all the spaces are uncovered.

About One Day   About One Second

About One Minute   About One Hour

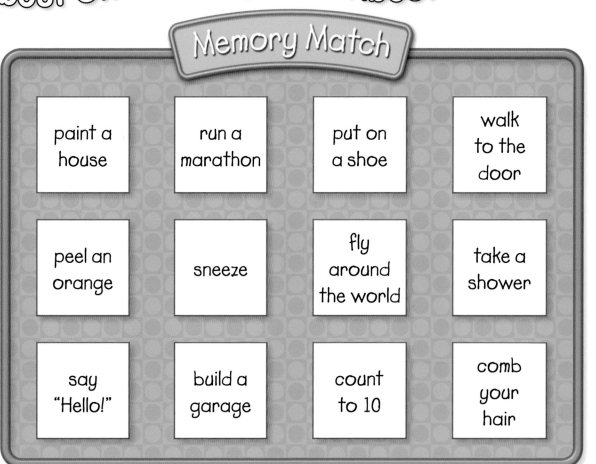

Memory Match

paint a house	run a marathon	put on a shoe	walk to the door
peel an orange	sneeze	fly around the world	take a shower
say "Hello!"	build a garage	count to 10	comb your hair

To win, collect the most squares.

Try Again Play again!

Partner Talk

Share your thinking while you work.

Try Together

Start 👫 Get a 🎲. Get 5 red squares. Take turns.

Try Toss the 🎲. Say the day next to your toss.
Put a square on every calendar space that shows that day.
Say the dates for those days. Remove the squares.
Take turns until each partner gets 6 or more turns.

January

⚀ Sunday

⚁ Monday

⚂ Tuesday

⚃ Wednesday

⚄ Thursday

⚅ Friday

Sunday	Monday	Tuesday	Wednesday	Thursday	Friday	Saturday
	1	2	3	4	5	6
7	8	9	10	11	12	13
14	15	16	17	18	19	20
21	22	23	24	25	26	27
28	29	30	31			

Try Again Take turns. Put a square in a calendar space.
Ask your partner to say the date one week earlier
or one week later.

Try Together

Partner Talk

Share your thinking while you work.

Start 👫 Get 🎲. Get a ⊂⊃. Take turns.

Try Choose a day on the calendar. Put a ⊂⊃ on the day you chose. Toss the 🎲. Follow the directions next to your toss. Repeat until each partner gets 6 or more turns.

September

Sunday	Monday	Tuesday	Wednesday	Thursday	Friday	Saturday
			1	2	3	4
5	6	7	8	9	10	11
12	13	14	15	16	17	18
19	20	21	22	23	24	25
26	27	28	29	30		

⚀ Give 2 facts about your day.

⚁ Name the day of the week.

⚂ Say the date for your day.

⚃ Tell how many days come before your day in that month.

⚄ Tell how many days come after your day in that month.

⚅ Say another date that is on the same day of the week.

Try Again This time, take turns. Put a ⊂⊃ in a calendar space. Ask your partner to say the date 2 weeks earlier or 2 weeks later.

Partner Talk

Share your thinking while you work.

Start 👫 Get 12 red squares. Cover each game space with a square. Take turns.

Try Uncover two game spaces. If you see the temperature and a word that matches the temperature, keep the squares. If not, put the squares back where they were. Take turns until all the spaces are uncovered.

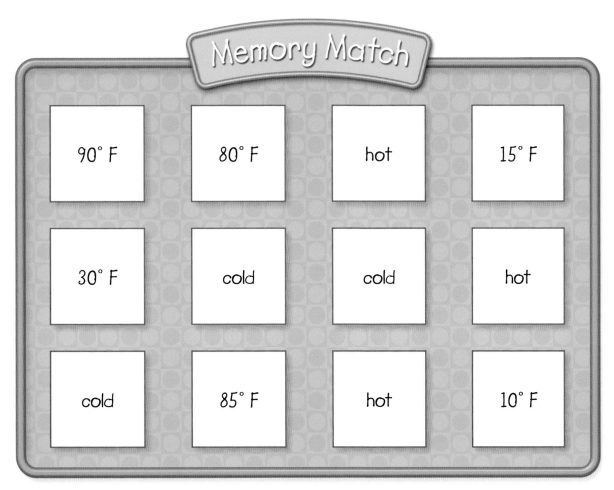

Memory Match

90° F	80° F	hot	15° F
30° F	cold	cold	hot
cold	85° F	hot	10° F

To win, collect the most squares.

Try Again Play again!

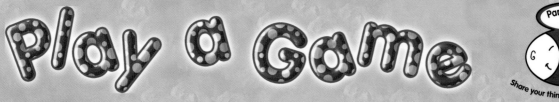

Play a Game

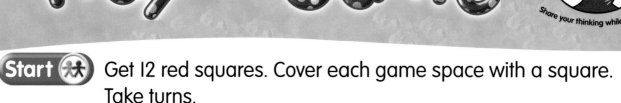

Share your thinking while you work.

Start Get 12 red squares. Cover each game space with a square. Take turns.

Try Uncover three game spaces. If you see a temperature, clothing for that temperature, and a word that matches that temperature, keep the squares. If not, put the squares back where they were. Take turns until all the spaces are uncovered.

Memory Match

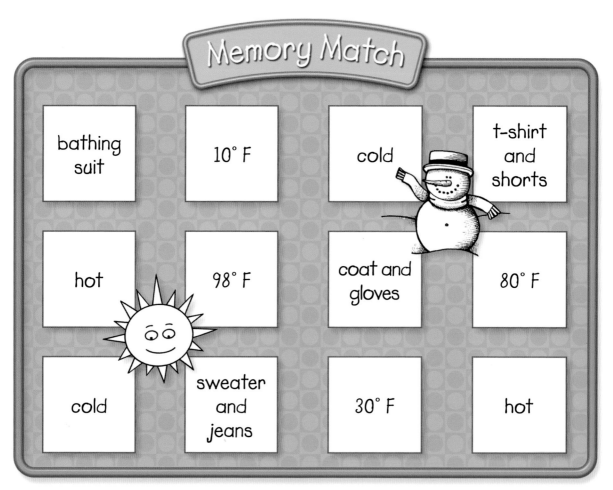

bathing suit	10° F	cold	t-shirt and shorts
hot	98° F	coat and gloves	80° F
cold	sweater and jeans	30° F	hot

To win, collect the most squares.

Try Again Play again!

Start  Put  in a 🛍️ .

Get a ⬭. Take turns.

Try Pick two tiles. Put them in the first two spaces. Ask your partner to pick two tiles and put them in the next two spaces. Read the story.

Flo looks over her homework. She decides it will take her

about ☐☐ minutes to write a story for

reading and about ☐☐ minutes to do math.

She has 45 minutes to work before dinner.

?

Use mental math. Find the amount of time Flo needs. Read the question. Put the ⬭ next to your answer.

When will Flo finish?

ahead of time		just on time		after dinner	

Try Again Remove the tiles and the ⬭. Repeat 8 times.
Change the time before dinner to one hour. Play again!

Try Together

Partner Talk

Share your thinking while you work.

Start 👥 Get  [0] [1] [2] [3] [4] [5] [6] [7] [8] [9] .

Get a 🎲. Take turns.

Try Read the story. Toss the 🎲. Read the end of the story next to that number. Work together. Choose number tiles. Put them in the empty spaces to get the ending you chose. Repeat 8 times.

Joe looks over his homework. He decides it will take about

minutes to finish a report and about

minutes to draw a map for Social Studies.

He has 55 minutes to work before dinner.

⚀	Joe finishes ahead of time.	⚄	Joe finishes ahead of time.
⚁	Joe finishes just on time.	⚄	Joe finishes just on time.
⚂	Joe has to work after dinner.	⚅	Joe has to work after dinner.

Try Again Change the time before dinner to one hour. Play again!

Look and See

Start 👥 Put  0 1 2 3 4 5 6 in a 🛍️.

Get 18 red squares.

Try Look at the list of favorite sports. Pick 4 tiles. Put them in the chart to show the number of children who voted for each sport.

Question

?

Fill in each blank with the name of a sport as you read this question. Then answer the question.

How many more children voted for _____
than for _____?

Soccer	Baseball	Tennis	Football
⚽	🏏	🎾	🏈

Use squares to make a graph for your data.

Favorite Sports Chosen by Second Graders

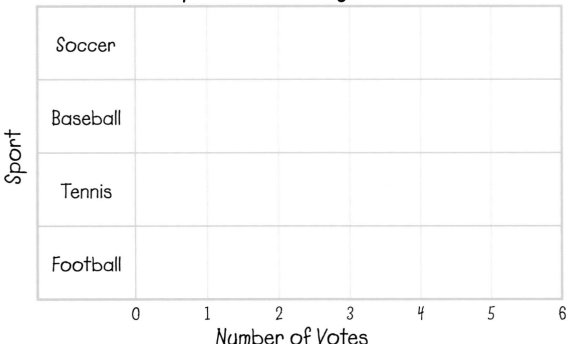

Sport

	0	1	2	3	4	5	6
Soccer							
Baseball							
Tennis							
Football							

Number of Votes

Try Again Pick tiles again. Put new data in the chart.
Repeat the activity with your new data.

Look and See

Partner Talk

Share your thinking while you work.

Start 👥 Get ⬜0 ⬜1 ⬜2 ⬜3 ⬜4 ⬜5 ⬜6 ⬜7 . Get 20 red squares.

Try Choose **A** or **B**. Read the clues.
Show the data in the chart with tiles.
Then make a bar graph to show that data.

A There are seven sunflowers. There are two daisies. There are three more tulips than daisies. There are 18 flowers in all.

B There are six daisies. There are five fewer tulips than daisies. There is one more rose than daisies. There are 19 flowers in all.

FLOWERS	
ROSES	
DAISIES	
TULIPS	
SUNFLOWER	

Flowers in the Garden

Flower		0	1	2	3	4	5	6	7
Rose									
Daisy									
Tulip									
Sunflower									

Number of Flowers

Try Again Use number tiles 0 – 6 to put data in the chart.
Then use that data to make a bar graph.

Look and See

Partner Talk

Share your thinking while you work.

Start  Put ⓪ ① ② ③ ④ ⑤ ⑥ ⑦ in a 🛍.

Look at the pictograph. Talk about the number of insects Jill counted in the park.

Try Take turns. Pick a tile. Put it at the bottom of the page. Ask your partner to read the question that has that answer. Decide if your partner is correct. Repeat until the 🛍 is empty.

Insects Jill Counted in the Park	
🐜 Ant	🐜 🐜 🐜 🐜 🐜 🐜
🦋 Butterfly	🦋 🦋 🦋 🦋 🦋
🐞 Ladybug	🐞 🐞 🐞 🐞 🐞 🐞 🐞
🐝 Bee	🐝 🐝 🐝 🐝

a. How many more ladybugs than ants did Jill count?

b. How many ladybugs did Jill count?

c. How many butterflies did Jill count?

d. How many fewer bees than ladybugs did Jill count?

e. How many more ants than bees did Jill count?

f. How many spiders did Jill count in the park?

g. How many ants did Jill count?

h. How many bees did Jill count?

The answer is ☐.

Try Again Take turns. Make up your own question. Ask your partner to answer your question.

Look and See

Partner Talk

Share your thinking while you work.

Start 🏃 Put ⓪ ① ② ③ ④ ⑤ ⑥ ⑦ in a 🛍.

Look at the pictograph. Talk about the number of insects Tom counted in the park.

Try Take turns. Pick a tile. Put it at the bottom of the page to make a two-digit number. Ask your partner to read the question that has that answer. Decide if your partner is correct. Repeat until the 🛍 is empty.

Insects Tom Counted in the Park	
🐜 Ant	🐜 🐜 🐜 🐜
🦋 Butterfly	🦋 🦋 🦋 🦋 🦋 🦋
🐞 Ladybug	🐞 🐞 🐞 🐞 🐞 🐞 🐞
🐝 Bee	🐝 🐝 🐝 🐝 🐝

a. How many ladybugs and bees did Tom count all together?

b. The next day, Tom counted twice as many ladybugs. How many did he count?

c. How many butterflies and ants did Tom count all together?

d. How many ladybugs, bees, and ants did Tom count all together?

e. How many butterflies, bees, and ants did Tom count all together?

f. How many butterflies and bees did Tom count all together?

g. How many ladybugs and butterflies did Tom count all together?

h. How many ladybugs, ants, and butterflies did Tom count all together?

The answer is 1☐.

Try Again Take turns. Make up your own question so that the answer is a word and not a number. Ask your partner to answer your question.

Try Together

Partner Talk

Share your thinking while you work.

Start 🚶 Get 6 red squares.

Try Look at the tally chart and the bar graph. Both show data from a survey of second graders' favorite beverages at lunch time. Answer each question. Use squares to cover the answers you do not choose.

Beverages	
Milk	卌 |||
Orange Juice	|||
Water	||||
Apple Juice	||

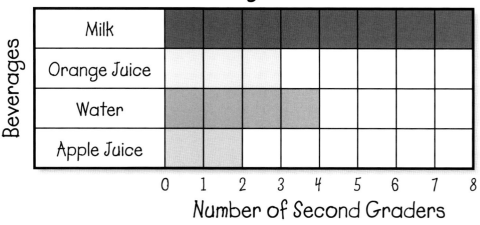

Favorite Beverages At Lunch Time

Beverages: Milk, Orange Juice, Water, Apple Juice

Number of Second Graders: 0 1 2 3 4 5 6 7 8

1. Which is the second graders' favorite beverage?

   [Orange Juice] [Milk] [Water]

2. How many children chose juice?

   [3] [2] [5]

3. Apple juice is the least favorite. Suppose three more children chose apple juice. Would it still be the least favorite?

   [YES] [NO]

4. How many children voted for their favorite beverage?

   [8] [17]

Try Again Take turns. Make up a question about the graph. Ask your partner to answer the question.

Try Together

Partner Talk

Share your thinking while you work.

Start 🤸 Get ⬜1⬜ ⬜1⬜ ⬜2⬜ ⬜2⬜ ⬜3⬜ ⬜3⬜ ⬜4⬜ ⬜4⬜.

Get 16 red squares.

Try Billy has a collection of favorite things in a shoe box. He empties the box and counts the items. Show his data with number tiles in the chart. Use squares to complete the bar graph.

Collection	
Marbles	
Shells	
Pencils	
Rings	

MY THINGS

Billy's Collection

Favorite Things

Marbles				
Shells				
Pencils				
Rings				

0   1   2   3   4

Number of Things

Use a number tile to answer each question.

1. How many more marbles are there than pencils?

2. How many pencils and rings are there?

Try Again Put different number tiles in the chart. Make a bar graph. Ask each other questions about the graph.

Look and See

Partner Talk

Share your thinking while you work.

Start 🚶 Get 8 red squares. Take turns.

Try Mom does many errands during her busy day. Locate one of her stops. Name the ordered pair at that location. Cover that location with a square. Take turns until every location is covered.

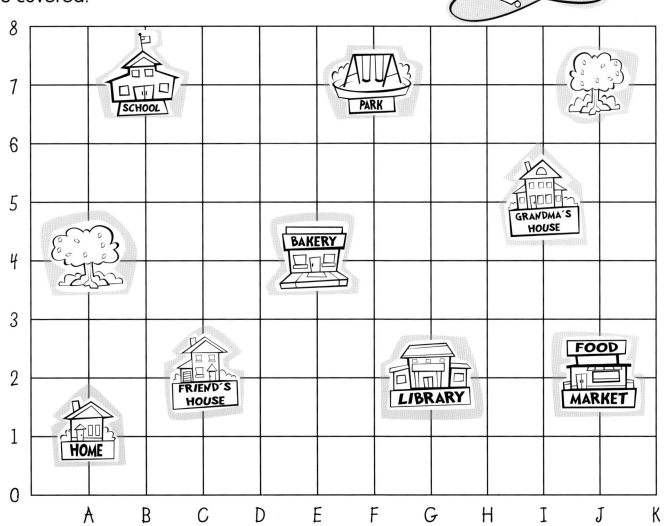

Try Again Remove the squares. Take turns.
On your turn, name an ordered pair.
Ask your partner to tell what is located at that point.

Look and See

Partner Talk

Share your thinking while you work.

Start 👫 Get 8 red squares. Cover each ordered pair with a red square. Work together.

Try Uncover an ordered pair. Locate that point on the grid. Put your square on that point. Work together until all the ordered pairs are uncovered.

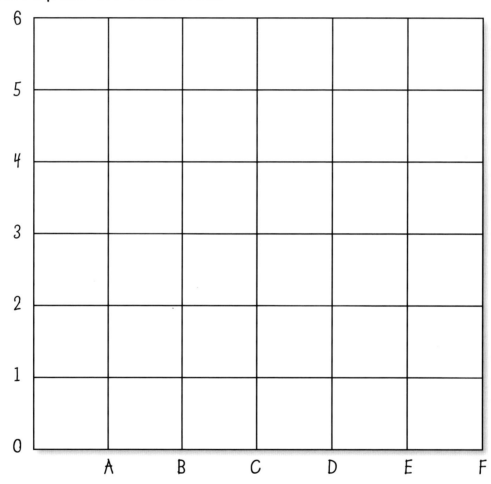

(C,5) (D,4) (B,2) (E,3) (C,1) (A,3) (D,2) (B,4)

Try Again Remove the squares. Take turns. On your turn, name eight ordered pairs. Each time you name an ordered pair, ask your partner to locate that point and cover it with a square. Try to make a design or a letter.

Start 👥 Get a . Get a 🛍.

Get 6 red squares and 6 blue squares for Player 1.
Get 7 red squares and 7 blue squares for Player 2.

Try PLAYER 1 Toss the 🎲. Put that number of red squares in the 🛍.

Toss the 🎲 again.
Put that number of blue squares in the 🛍.
Predict: What color are you more likely to pick?

Shake the 🛍. Pick a square.
Hold it up so Player 2 can see it.
Ask Player 2 to show what you picked by filling a
space below. Put the square back in the 🛍.

Keep picking until Player 2 fills a complete row.
Check: Did you get what you predicted?

PLAYER 2

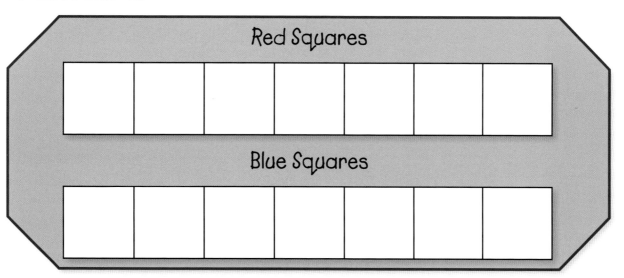

Red Squares

Blue Squares

Try Again This time, change jobs with your partner.

Try Together

Partner Talk

Share your thinking while you work.

Start 🧍 Get 7 red squares.
Use squares to cover the colors on every bag. Take turns.

Try Remove a square. Read what is in the bag.
Choose a prediction for picking a color from that bag.
Use the square to cover your prediction.

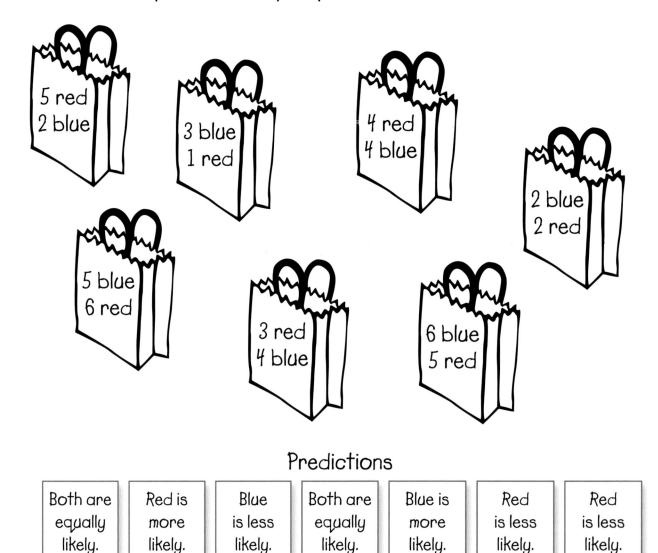

5 red
2 blue

3 blue
1 red

4 red
4 blue

2 blue
2 red

5 blue
6 red

3 red
4 blue

6 blue
5 red

Predictions

| Both are equally likely. | Red is more likely. | Blue is less likely. | Both are equally likely. | Blue is more likely. | Red is less likely. | Red is less likely. |

Try Again This time, begin by covering every prediction.
Then play the opposite way.

Math in Motion

Partner Talk
Share your thinking while you work.

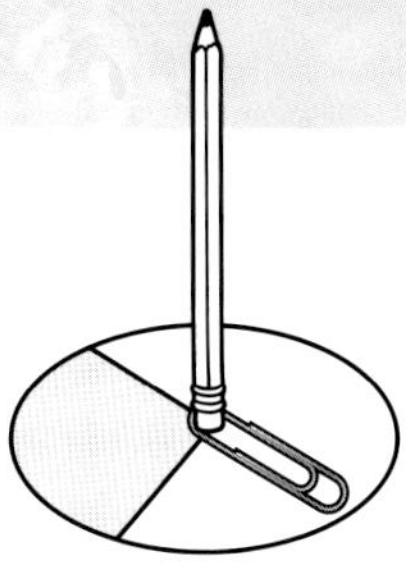

Start Get 9 red squares. Get 6 blue squares.
Get a 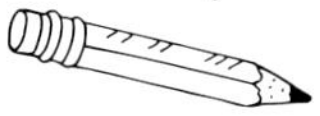. Get a large 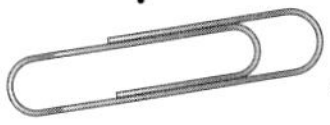.
Work together.

Try

Choose a circle.

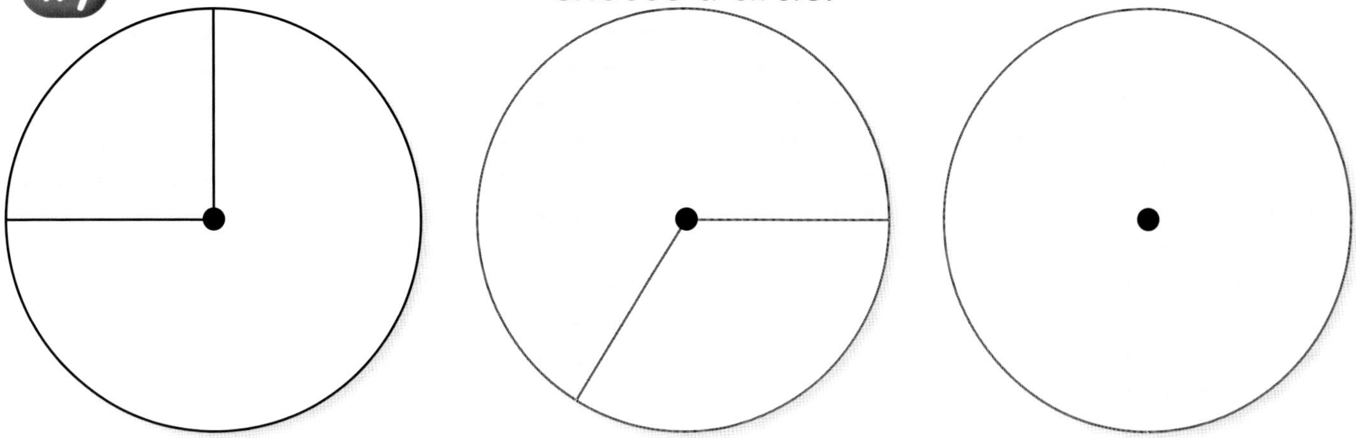

Tell what might happen if you spin the 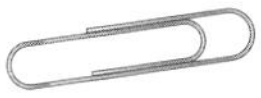 on the circle nine times.
Put a blue square in front of each answer you choose.

☐ Certain to stop on grey	☐ More probable to stop on white	☐ Less probable to stop on grey
☐ Impossible to stop on white	☐ More probable to stop on grey	☐ Less probable to stop on white

Spin nine times. Each time you spin,
put a red square on the graph to record the result.

White									
Grey									

Look at your results and the answers you chose. Do they match?

Try Again Begin again! This time, use a different spinner.

Math in Motion

Partner Talk

Share your thinking while you work.

Start 🚶 Get 20 red squares. Get 20 blue squares.
Get a 🛍 for the squares. Get a 🎲. Take turns.

Try Toss the 🎲. Follow the directions next to that toss.
Then give all the other squares to your partner.

⚁ Fill the 🛍 with 10 squares so it is probable you will pick more blue squares.

⚀ Fill the 🛍 with 10 squares so that it is probable you will pick more red squares.

⚂ Fill the 🛍 with 10 squares so it is impossible to pick a blue square.

⚃ Fill the 🛍 with 10 squares so that it is certain you will pick a blue square.

⚄ Fill the 🛍 with 10 squares so it is probable you will pick fewer red squares.

⚅ Fill the 🛍 with 10 squares so that picking a red square and picking a blue square are equally likely.

Cover your eyes. Pick a square from the 🛍. Let your partner record your pick on the graph. Put the square back in the 🛍. Pick and let your partner record nine more times. Talk about your results.

Red									
Blue									

Try Again Begin again!

 **Play a Game**

Partner Talk
Share your thinking while you work.

Start 🏃 Get 1 red square and a ⬭ to use as game markers. Get a 🎲. Get 20 blue squares. Give one game marker to each player. Take turns.

Try Toss the 🎲. Move your marker that number of game spaces. Think of a question you can ask about the graph so that the answer is the number your marker is on. If you ask a question, collect one blue square. If not, stay on that space but do not collect a square.

Start Here!
↓

			12	80	5
4			Miss a Turn		14
7		3	10		6
8	32	Free			8

| | | 20 | 14 |
| | | | Miss a Turn |

Colored Buttons

Red					
Yellow					
Green					
Orange					
Blue					

0 2 4 6 8 10 12
Number in One Bag

Finish

| 6 | 10 | 80 | 2 | Free | 12 | 40 |

To win, collect the most blue squares!

Try Again Play again!

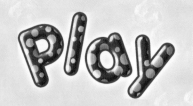 # Play a Game

Partner Talk

Share your thinking while you work.

Start Get 1 red square and a ⬯ to use as game markers. Get a 🎲. Get 20 blue squares. Give one game marker to each player. Take turns.

Try Toss the 🎲. Move your marker that number of game spaces. Think of a question you can ask about the graphs so that the answer is the number your marker is on. If you ask a question, collect one blue square. If not, stay on your game space, but do not collect a square.

Start Here! ↓

	3	18	5

| 6 | | 9 | Miss a Turn |

| 12 | 6 | 24 | 2 |

| 3 | Free | 1 | 6 |

| | | | 54 |

| | | | 12 |

Finish

| 5 | 15 | 24 | Miss a Turn | 15 | 3 |

Colored Buttons

Green						
Yellow						
Red						
Blue						
Orange						

0 3 6 9 12 15 18

Number in One Bag

Buttons Needed for a Rag Doll

Eyes					
Nose					
Ears					
Buttons					
Mouth					

0 1 2 3 4 5 6

Number for One Doll

To win, collect the most blue squares!

Try Again Play again!

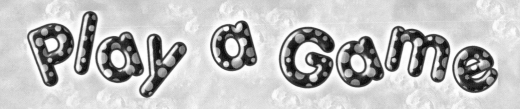

Share your thinking while you work.

 Put 0 1 2 3 4 5 6 7 8 9 in a 📄.

Get 18 red squares. Give one game board to each player. Read the three-digit numbers on your game board to your partner. Take turns.

Try Pick a tile. Cover a matching digit on your game board if you see it there. Put the tile back in the 📄.

hundreds	tens	ones
3	4	6
9	7	0
2	8	5

hundreds	tens	ones
4	9	1
8	5	0
7	3	6

To win, get ■ ■ ■ and then say that number correctly.

Try Again Remove the squares. Play again! Talk about the number of hundreds, tens and ones in each number.

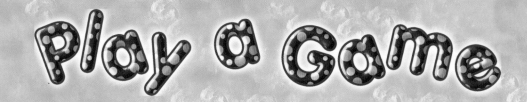

Partner
Talk

Share your thinking while you work.

Give one game board to each player. Read the three-digit numbers on your game board to your partner.
Say how many hundreds, tens and ones are in each number.

Try Pick a tile.
Cover a matching digit on your game board if you see it there.
Put the tile back in the 🛍️.

7 hundreds	2 ones	1 ten
5 tens	0 hundreds	6 ones
3 ones	4 tens	9 hundreds

9 tens	2 hundreds	7 ones
8 ones	3 tens	1 hundred
4 hundreds	0 ones	6 tens

To win, get ■ ■ ■ or ■ and say that number correctly.

Try Again Put the tiles back in the 🛍️. Play again!
This time use the other game board.

Try Together

Share your thinking while you work.

Start 👥 Put [0] [1] [2] [3] [4] [5] [6] [7] [8] [9]

and [0] [1] [2] [3] [4] [5] [6] [7] [8] [9] in a 🛍️ .

Try together.

Try Pick three tiles. Put them in the spaces below. Say that number. Farmer Fred picks that number of apples from his trees. Ask your partner to point to the number of boxes of 100, packs of 10, and single apples Farmer Fred has.

Hundreds	Tens	Ones

Box of 100 apples — **100 Apples**

Pack of 10 apples — **10 Apples**

1 apple —

100 Apples **100 Apples** **100 Apples** **100 Apples** **100 Apples** **100 Apples**

100 Apples **100 Apples** **100 Apples**

10 Apples   10 Apples   10 Apples   10 Apples   10 Apples

10 Apples   10 Apples   10 Apples   10 Apples

Try Again Begin again! This time, point to some boxes of 100, packs of 10, and single apples. Ask your partner to use number tiles to show how many apples Farmer Fred has.

Center Activity 17-2 ⭐

Partner Talk

Share your thinking while you work.

Try Together

Start 👥 Get [0] [1] [2] [3] [4] [5] [6] [7] [8] [9].

Get a ⬭. Get a ✏️. Take turns.

Try Spin the ⬭ on the circle. Use tiles to make a number that fits the directions.

Example:
Spin "more than 600."
Make 731.

Hundreds	Tens	Ones

Ask your partner to point to all the numbers that come after your number.

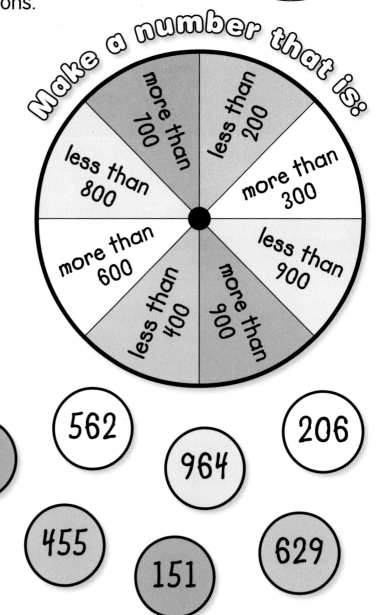

Make a number that is:

more than 700 · less than 200 · more than 300 · less than 900 · more than 900 · less than 400 · more than 600 · less than 800

375   798   562   206
327   964
444   455   629
990   837   151

Try Again Begin again! This time, ask your partner to point to all the numbers that come before your number.

Try Together

Partner Talk
Share your thinking while you work.

Start 👫 Put 0 1 2 3 4 5 6 7 8 9 in a 🛍.

Take turns.

Try Pick 3 tiles. Ask your partner to help you place those tiles in the squares to make the greatest number possible.
Tap on the place value blocks to show that number.
Take turns saying the number in expanded form and standard form.

Example 5 hundreds 4 tens 3 ones

Say 500 + 40 + 3, five hundred forty-three.

☐ hundreds + ☐ tens + ☐ ones

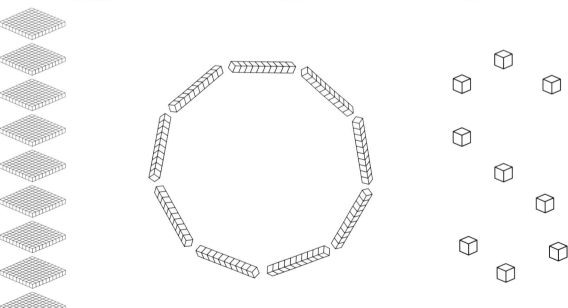

Try Again Put the tiles back in the 🛍.
Repeat until each player gets 5 turns.

Try Together

Partner Talk

Share your thinking while you work.

Start 👫 Put ⓪ ① ② ③ ④ ⑤ ⑥ ⑦ ⑧ ⑨ in a 🛍.

Try Each player takes out 2 tiles from the 🛍. Together, decide which 3 of your 4 tiles will make the greatest number. Put them in the spaces below. Tap on the place value blocks to show that number.
Take turns saying the number in expanded form and standard form.

Example ⑤ hundreds ④ tens ③ ones

Say 500 + 40 + 3, five hundred forty-three.

| | hundreds + | | tens + | | ones |

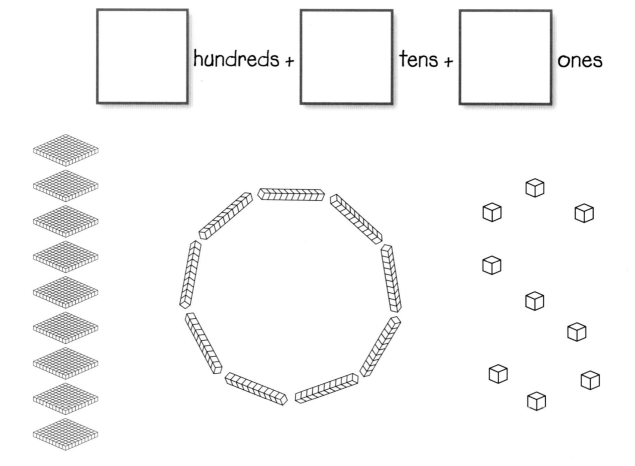

Try Again Put the tiles back in the 🛍.
Repeat until each player gets 5 turns.

Try Together

Start 👥 Get 20 red squares. Take turns.

Try Point to a space that has an addition or a subtraction sign.
Ask your partner what you should add or subtract.
Point to those blocks. Work together to find the space with the answer.
Cover both spaces.

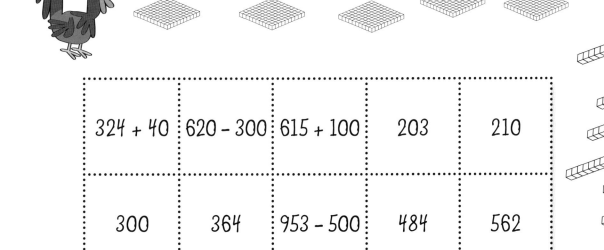

324 + 40	620 – 300	615 + 100	203	210
300	364	953 – 500	484	562
453	542 + 20	290 + 10	147 + 50	320
404 + 80	260 – 50	715	197	200 + 3

Play until all the spaces are covered.

Try Again Remove the squares. Play again.

Try Together

Partner Talk

Share your thinking while you work.

Start 👫 Get 10 blue squares for one player. Get 10 red squares for the other player. Take turns.

Try Point to a game space. Explain how to add or subtract. Say the answer. Ask your partner to find another problem that has the same answer. Explain why the problems have the same answer. Cover both spaces.

953 – 500	360 + 4	200 + 3	200 + 100	414+70
290 + 10	620 – 300	250 – 40	853 – 400	137 + 60
615 + 100	542 + 20	420 – 100	324 + 40	183 + 20
515 + 200	260 – 50	462 + 100	404 + 80	147 + 50

Play until all the spaces are covered.

Try Again Remove the squares. Play again.

Listen and Learn

Start 👥 Place 3 red squares and 3 blue squares in a . Take turns.

Try Pick a square. Place it on a matching space below. Ask your partner to recite the number pattern starting at the step next to your colored square.

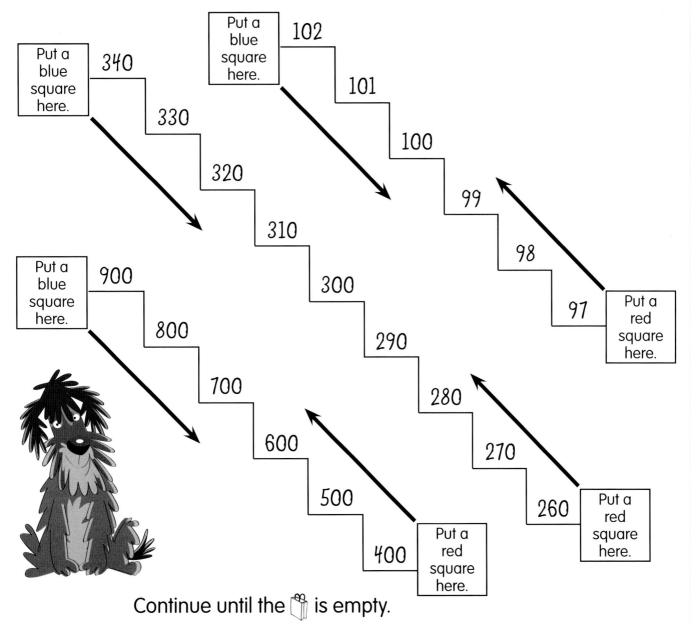

Continue until the 🛍 is empty.

Try Again Put the squares back in the 🛍. Repeat.

Listen and Learn

Start Place 3 red squares and 3 blue squares in a 🛍. Take turns.

Try Pick a square. Place it on a matching space below.
Ask your partner to recite the number pattern starting at
the step next to your colored square. Take turns until the 🛍 is empty.

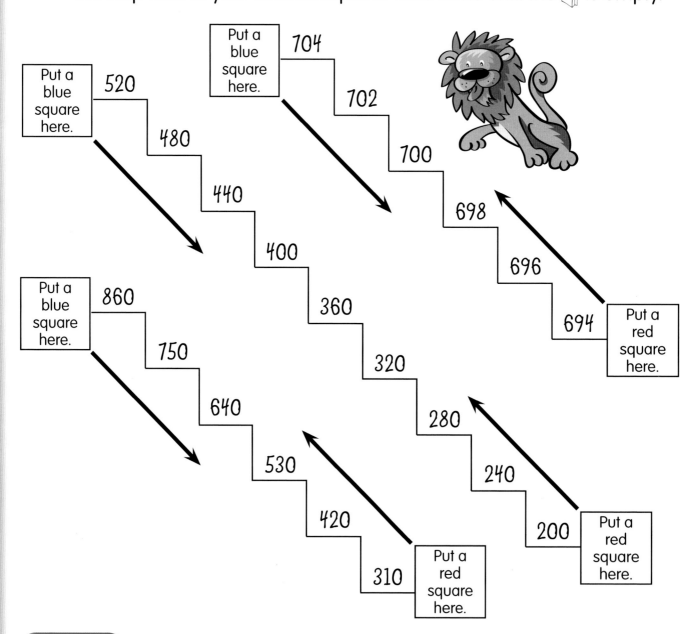

Try Again Talk about the patterns. Which number would be next at the
top and bottom of each staircase?

Listen and Learn

Partner Talk

Share your thinking while you work.

Start 👫 Get  0 1 2 3 4 5 6 7 8 9 .

Try Get a pencil. Work together.

Choose 3 tiles. Make a three-digit number to the left of <.
Let your partner choose 3 tiles for the other three-digit number.

			<			

Using the end of the pencil with the eraser, tap on
the place-value blocks to show each number.

Say: _____ is less than _____ .

Trace < when you say "is less than".

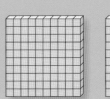

Choose 3 tiles. Make a three-digit number to the left of >.
Let your partner choose 3 tiles for the other three-digit number.

			>			

Using the end of the pencil with the eraser, tap on
the place-value blocks to show each number.

Say: _____ is greater than _____ .

Trace > when you say "is greater than".

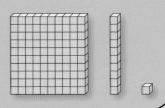

Try Again Remove the tiles. Try each puzzle again.

Partner Talk
Share your thinking while you work.

Listen and Learn

Start 👫 Get  0 1 2 3 4 5 6 7 8 9 .

Try

Choose six tiles. Show two 3-digit numbers here.
Make sure that the number on the left is less.

[ ] [ ] [ ] < [ ] [ ] [ ]

Say: _____ is less than _____ .

Trace < when you say "is less than".

Ask your partner to put your tiles in a different order here.
Make sure that the number on the left is greater.

[ ] [ ] [ ] > [ ] [ ] [ ]

Say: _____ is greater than _____ .

Trace > when you say "is greater than".

Try Again Remove the tiles. Try again.
This time, tap on the place-value blocks
to show your partner which two numbers to make.

Start 👥 Get 15 red squares.
Cover each game space with a square. Take turns.

Try Uncover three game spaces.

If you see a number that is between the other two numbers and one away from each, keep the squares.

If not, put the squares back where they were.
Take turns until all the spaces are uncovered.

Memory Match

152	543	157	416	542
415	523	153	524	417
156	525	158	154	541

To win, collect the most squares.

Try Again Play again!

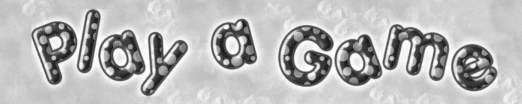

Partner Talk

Share your thinking while you work.

Start 👥 Get 15 red squares.
Cover each game space with a square. Take turns.

Try Uncover three game spaces.

If you see a number that is between the other two numbers and one away from each, keep the squares.

If not, put the squares back where they were.
Take turns until all the spaces are uncovered.

Memory Match

99	991	998	301	699
990	100	300	1,000	101
299	989	698	999	700

To win, collect the most squares.

Try Again Play again!

Try Together

Partner Talk
Share your thinking while you work.

Start 👫 Get [0] [1] [2] [3] [4] [5] [6] [7] [8] [9].

Work together.

Try Use 6 tiles. Show a number that is less than the middle number. Show a number that is greater than the middle number.

┌──┬──┬──┐   ┌──┬──┬──┐
│ │ │ │ ,357, │ │ │ │
└──┴──┴──┘   └──┴──┴──┘
   Least   Greatest

Ask your partner to rearrange your tiles to show a different way to solve the puzzle.

Now try these puzzles.

┌──┬──┬──┐   ┌──┬──┬──┐
│ │ │ │ ,289, │ │ │ │
└──┴──┴──┘   └──┴──┴──┘
   Least   Greatest

┌──┬──┬──┐   ┌──┬──┬──┐
│ │ │ │ ,450, │ │ │ │
└──┴──┴──┘   └──┴──┴──┘
   Least   Greatest

Try Again This time, choose your own middle number.

Try Together

Start 👥 Get ⌈0⌉ ⌈1⌉ ⌈2⌉ ⌈3⌉ ⌈4⌉ ⌈5⌉ ⌈6⌉ ⌈7⌉ ⌈8⌉ ⌈9⌉. Take turns.

Try Find three different ways to solve each puzzle.

Use ⌈3⌉, ⌈4⌉ and ⌈9⌉ in this puzzle.

349, 439, [ ][ ][ ]
Least   Greatest

Use ⌈1⌉, ⌈2⌉ and ⌈7⌉ in this puzzle.

127, [ ][ ][ ] , 721
Least   Greatest

Use ⌈5⌉, ⌈6⌉ and ⌈8⌉ in this puzzle.

[ ][ ][ ] , 685, 865
Least   Greatest

Try Again Make up your own puzzle.

Listen and Learn

Partner Talk

Share your thinking while you work.

Start 🚶 Get ① ② ③ ④ .

Get ⬭ ⬭ ⬭ .
Work together.

Try Point to a train. Look at the numbers. The numbers on the train cars got out of order. Say the numbers in order from least to greatest. Put a number tile under each car to show the order. Then talk about the pattern. Put a ⬭ below the conductor who has the rule for the pattern.

Try Again Play again! This time, tell which numbers would be on the next two cars in each train.

Listen and Learn

Partner Talk

Share your thinking while you work.

Start 👫 Get ⬜1️⃣ ⬜2️⃣ ⬜3️⃣ ⬜4️⃣.

Get 📎 📎 📎 📎.
Work together.

Try Point to an airplane. The numbers behind it got out of order. Say the numbers in order from least to greatest. Put a number tile below each number to show the order. Talk about the pattern. Put a 📎 below the cloud that shows the rule for the pattern. Then say the next two numbers in the list.

| 150 | 210 | 180 | 120 | ? | ? |

| 800 | 700 | 750 | 850 | ? | ? |

| 189 | 199 | 179 | 209 | ? | ? |

| 220 | 140 | 180 | 100 | ? | ? |

☁ +10   ☁ +40   ☁ +30   ☁ +50

Try Again This time, say the next five numbers that would be in each list.

Start 👫 Put ⬚1 ⬚2 ⬚3 ⬚4 ⬚5 in a 🛍️. Get 18 red squares.

Get a ⬭. Give one game board to each player.
Play at the same time.

Try Place a ⬭ below one of these numbers.

216 ....

425 ....

Pick a tile. Put it here.

Add ⬚ hundreds

Explain how to add that number of hundreds to the number you chose. Any player who has the sum covers it with a square. Put the tile back in the 🛍️. Repeat until one player wins.

Four Corners

525	316	725
825	516	925
416	625	616

Four Corners

516	716	925
625	316	525
416	825	616

To win, be the first player to cover four corners.

Try Again Play again!

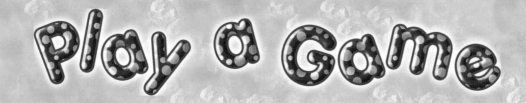 Play a Game

Partner Talk
Share your thinking while you work.

Start 👫 Put ⓵ ② ③ ④ ⑤ ⑥ in a 🛍. Get 18 red squares.

Get a ⬭. Give one game board to each player.
Play at the same time.

Try Place a ⬭ below
one of these numbers.

164   378

Pick a tile. Put it here.

Add ☐ hundreds

Explain how to add that number of hundreds to the number
you chose. Any player who has the sum covers it with a square.
Put the tile back in the 🛍. Repeat until one player wins.

Four Corners

264	564	478
678	578	364
464	978	878

Four Corners

778	878	364
664	478	764
678	564	978

To win, be the first player to cover four corners.

Try Again Play again!

Partner Talk

Share your thinking while you work.

Start 🚶 Get 20 red squares for one player.

Get 20 blue squares for the other player.

Get a 🎲. Take turns.

Try Toss the 🎲. Count that number of spaces on the game board. Estimate the sum of the two numbers in each space. Use hundreds and tens to help you say: *The number in all is more than _____.* After you do this, cover each space with a square.

 Start Here!
⬇

Cover the Path!

		440	111	333	807
150 **357**		360	222	444	109

184 **372**		677 240			209 366

271 **189**		222 111	150 395		444 444

122 **561**	301 499	509 405			121 212	330 440

						250 457

To win, put the most squares on the path!

414 357	212 313	407 328	567 189	770 102	350 357	190 437

Try Again Play again!

Play a Game

Partner Talk
Share your thinking while you work.

Start 👥 Put ⓵②③④⑤ and ⓵②③④⑤ in a 🛍️.

Get 20 red squares for one player.
Get 20 blue squares for the other player. Take turns.

Try Pick 6 number tiles from the 🛍️. Put them here.

			+			

Explain how to estimate the sum. If the estimate is less than 800, put 1 square on the path. If the estimate is more than 800, put 2 squares on the path.

Start Here! ↓

Cover the Path!

To win, put the most squares on the path!

Try Again Play again!

Center Activity 18-2 ⭐ ⭐

Partner Talk

Share your thinking while you work.

Try Together

Start 🧒🧒 Get 1 2 3 4 5 6 7 8 9 .

Get place-value blocks. Or get 📝 to draw blocks. Work together.

Try Explain how to add. Use number tiles to show the sum.

H	T	O
3	2	5
4	6	1
+		

H	T	O
1	1	9
1	2	6
+		

H	T	O
4	0	4
5	0	9
+		

Try Again Create another addition problem. Explain how to add your numbers.

Try Together

Partner Talk

Share your thinking while you work.

Start 👬 Get ①②③④⑤⑥⑦⑧⑨.

Get place-value blocks. Or get 📝 to draw blocks.
Work together.

Try Explain how to add. Use number tiles to show the sum.

H	T	O
4	5	8
4	6	6

+

H	T	O
1	9	5
1	6	2

+

H	T	O
2	8	3
3	9	8

+

Try Again Create another addition problem.
Explain how to add your numbers.

Play a Game

Start Get ⬜1 ⬜2 ⬜3 ⬜4 ⬜5 ⬜6 .

Get 18 red squares. Get ✏️. Give one game board to each player. Play at the same time.

Try Make a number with
⬜1 , ⬜2 , and ⬜3 .
Show it here. ➡️

Make a number with
⬜4 , ⬜5 , and ⬜6 .
Show it here. ➡️

H	T	O
+		

Explain how to add. Any player who has the sum covers it with a square. Repeat until one player wins.

Four Corners

588	768	669
858	777	786
597	696	975

Four Corners

687	678	759
867	966	795
876	885	957

To win, be the first player to cover four corners.

Try Again Play again!

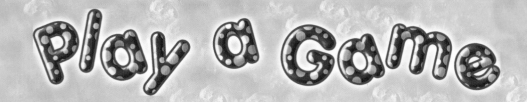

Partner Talk

Share your thinking while you work.

Start  Get ⬜1 ⬜2 ⬜3 ⬜4 ⬜5 ⬜6 .

Get 18 red squares. Get 🖊️. Give one game board to each player. Play at the same time.

Try Make a number with
⬜1 , ⬜2 , and ⬜3 .
Show it here. ➡️

Make a number with
⬜4 , ⬜5 , and ⬜6 .
Show it here. ➡️

H	T	O
+		

Estimate the sum. Any player who has the sum covers it with a square. Repeat until one player wins.

Four Corners

957	678	795
966	867	759
885	876	687

Four Corners

768	588	777
858	669	786
696	975	597

To win, be the first player to cover four corners.

Try Again Play again!

Listen and Learn

Start  Put  in a . Work together.

Try

> Trace the arrows as you count on from 380 to 720.
> Ask your partner to say the missing part of 720.
>
> 380 + _____ = 720

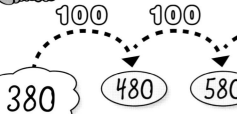

| 100 | 100 | 100 | 10 | 10 | 10 | 10 |

380   480   580   680   690   700   710   720

> Trace the arrows as you count back from 680 to 450.
> Ask your partner to say the missing part of 680.
>
> 450 + _____ = 680

| 10 | 10 | 10 | 100 | 100 |

450   460   470   480   580   680

Pick two tiles. Put them in the empty spaces. Say the 3-digit number.
Count on or count back. Find the missing part of 700.

| | | **0** |

0 + _____ = 700

Try Again  Put the tiles back in the . Repeat the activity.

Listen and Learn

Start Put [3] [4] [5] [6] [7] in a .

Work together.

Try Choose A, B, or C. Pick 2 tiles. Put them in the empty spaces.

Count on 230 from your number. Say the sum.

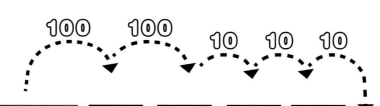

A [ ] [ ] **0** + 230 = _____

Count back 320 from your number. Say the missing part of your number.

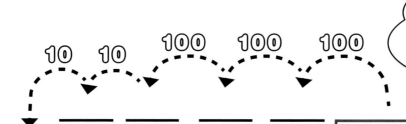

B _____ + 320 = [ ] [ ] **0**

Count on or count back to find the missing part of 900.

C [ ] [ ] **0** + _____ = 900

Try Again Put the tiles back in the . Repeat the activity.

Try Together

Partner Talk
Share your thinking while you work.

Start 🚶 Get ⬭⬭ and ⬭⬭.

Get ⬚0⬚ ⬚1⬚ ⬚2⬚ ⬚3⬚ ⬚4⬚ ⬚5⬚ ⬚6⬚ ⬚7⬚ ⬚8⬚ ⬚9⬚ .

Try Choose a number in the left column. Place a ⬭⬭ below it. Use tiles to show a 3-digit number that is close to the number you chose. Now choose a number from the right column. Place a ⬭⬭ below it. Use tiles to show a 3-digit number that is close to the number you chose.

About 900
⸳................⸳

About 400
⸳................⸳

About 800
⸳................⸳

About 300
⸳................⸳

About 700
⸳................⸳

About 200
⸳................⸳

About 600
⸳................⸳

About 100
⸳................⸳

About 500
⸳................⸳

			−			

Estimate. Say: The difference is about _____.

Try Again Explain how the number above each ⬭⬭ helps you to estimate.

Partner Talk

Share your thinking while you work.

Try Together

Start  Get ⓪ ① ② ③ ④ ⑤ ⑥ ⑦ ⑧ ⑨.

Get 8 red squares.

Try Point to an estimate.

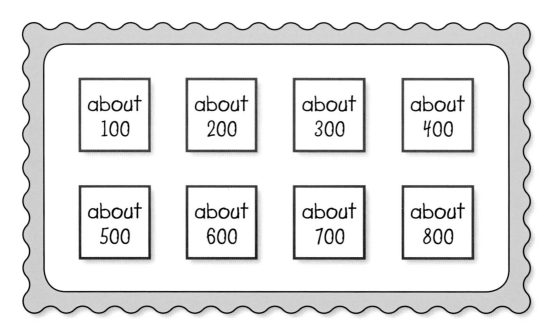

about 100   about 200   about 300   about 400

about 500   about 600   about 700   about 800

Use tiles to make a difference that is close to your estimate.

☐ ☐ ☐ **—** ☐ ☐ ☐

Explain why your difference is close to the estimate. Cover the estimate with a square. Repeat until every estimate is covered.

Try Again This time, play in reverse. First, use tiles to make two 3-digit numbers. Estimate the difference. Then cover the estimate. Repeat until every estimate is covered.

Look and See

Partner Talk

Share your thinking while you work.

Start 👥 Get ⌐1⌐ ⌐2⌐ ⌐3⌐ ⌐4⌐ ⌐5⌐ ⌐6⌐ ⌐7⌐ ⌐8⌐ ⌐9⌐ .

Get place-value blocks. Or get 📝 to draw blocks.

Try Choose **a, b, c,** or **d**. Explain how to subtract. Regroup if needed. Show the answer with tiles.

a

H	T	O
9	2	8
− 4	1	2

b

H	T	O
7	8	9
− 5	4	2

c

H	T	O
6	0	9
− 2	1	1

d

H	T	O
8	4	1
− 5	2	9

Try Again Use number tiles to make two 3-digit numbers. Estimate the difference.

Look and See

Start 👫 Get  0 1 2 3 4 5 6 7 8 9

and 0 1 2 3 4 5 6 7 8 9 .

Get place-value blocks. Or get 📝 to draw blocks.

Try Choose **a,** or **b**. Place one number tile below each digit. Use or draw place-value blocks. Explain how to subtract the two 3-digit numbers. Regroup if needed. Show your answer with tiles if possible.

a

H	T	O
5	1	2

Remember . . .
Subtract a number that is
less than 512!

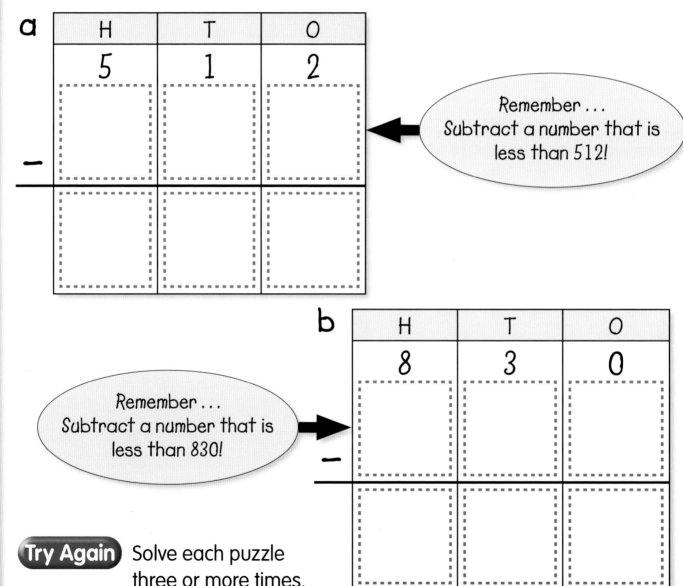

b

H	T	O
8	3	0

Remember . . .
Subtract a number that is
less than 830!

Try Again Solve each puzzle three or more times.

Center Activity 18-7 ⭐ ⭐

Start 🏃 Put ⓪ and ① in a 🛍️. Get 18 red squares.

Give one game board to each player. Take turns.

Try Pick a tile from the 🛍️. If you get ⓪, look on your game board.
Find a problem that does not require regrouping.
Explain why it does not. Cover it.

If you get ①, look on your game board.
Find a problem that requires regrouping.
Explain why it does. Cover it. Put the tile back in the 🛍️.
Repeat until one player wins.

Four Corners

349 − 125	465 − 283	637 − 524
265 − 104	572 − 345	339 − 146
758 − 129	985 − 193	892 − 751

Four Corners

732 − 219	526 − 317	345 − 126
483 − 163	934 − 723	485 − 154
654 − 382	561 − 460	827 − 203

To win, be the first player who covers four corners.

Try Again Play again!

Play a Game

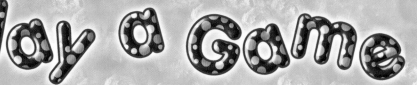

Partner Talk

Share your thinking while you work.

Start 🚶 Put ①②③④⑤⑥⑦⑧⑨ in a 🛍️ .

Get 18 red squares. Get place-value blocks.
Or get ✏️ to draw blocks. Give one game board
to each player. Play at the same time.

Try Pick a tile. Find the problem next to that tile number.
Explain how to subtract. Both players cover the difference.
Set the tile aside. Repeat until one player wins.

① $\begin{array}{r} 579 \\ -286 \end{array}$	② $\begin{array}{r} 542 \\ -361 \end{array}$	③ $\begin{array}{r} 635 \\ -111 \end{array}$	④ $\begin{array}{r} 639 \\ -527 \end{array}$	⑤ $\begin{array}{r} 321 \\ -119 \end{array}$
⑥ $\begin{array}{r} 946 \\ -199 \end{array}$	⑦ $\begin{array}{r} 789 \\ -485 \end{array}$	⑧ $\begin{array}{r} 799 \\ -389 \end{array}$	⑨ $\begin{array}{r} 596 \\ -418 \end{array}$	

Four Corners

304	178	747
112	181	410
202	524	293

Four Corners

181	112	524
747	202	293
410	304	178

To win, be the first player who covers four corners.

Try Again Play again!

Try Together

Partner Talk

Share your thinking while you work.

Start Get 20 red squares.

Try Read the data in the chart. Use squares to make a graph of the data. Then answer each question.

Book Fair Sales

Day of the Week	Story Books	Picture Books
Monday	150	200
Tuesday	250	150
Wednesday	200	50

a. On which day were the most books sold?

b. On which day were the fewest books sold?

c. How many more story books than picture books were sold on Wednesday?

d. How many books were sold on Monday and Wednesday?

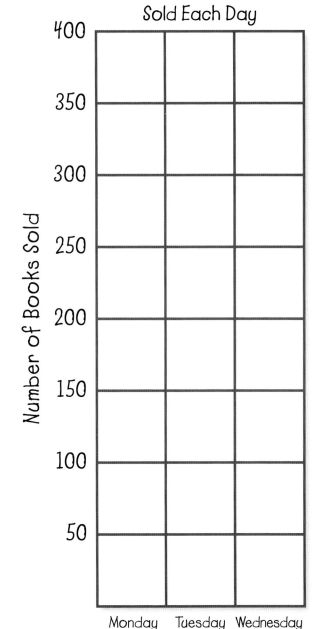

Number of Books Sold Each Day

Try Again Were more picture books or more story books sold at the fair?

Try Together

Partner Talk

Share your thinking while you work.

Start  Put ⬜1 ⬜1 ⬜2 ⬜2 in a 🛍️.
Get 20 red squares.

Try Pick one tile at a time. Fill all of the spaces in the chart on the left. Use squares to make a graph of the data. Then answer each question.

Number of People Who Attended the School Play

	Saturday	Sunday
Children	50	00
Adults	50	50

a. Did more adults or more children attend the play?

b. How many children attended the school play?

c. What is the difference between the number of adults and the number of children who attended on Sunday?

d. How many people attended the play on Saturday?

Try Again Put the tiles back in the 🛍️.
Remove the squares. Play again!

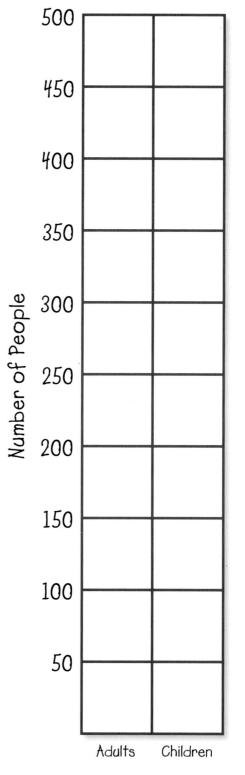

Number of People Who Attended the School Play

Number of People
500
450
400
350
300
250
200
150
100
50

Adults   Children

Cover Three

Partner Talk

Share your thinking while you work.

Start 🚶 Put [2] [3] [4] [5] in a 🛍.

Get 10 red squares. Get 10 blue squares. Take turns.

Try Pick 2 tiles. Put them in the blank squares. Explain how to find the number of oranges in all.

If you see the answer on the game board, cover it.

If the answer is taken, lose your turn.

Put the tiles back in the 🛍.

☐ baskets

☐ oranges in each basket

How many oranges in all?

4 + 4 2 times 4 8 in all	3 + 3 + 3 + 3 4 times 3 12 in all	2 + 2 + 2 + 2 + 2 5 times 2 10 in all
4 + 4 + 4 + 4 + 4 5 times 4 20 in all	5 + 5 + 5 3 times 5 15 in all	3 + 3 2 times 3 6 in all
5 + 5 + 5 + 5 4 times 5 20 in all	3 + 3 + 3 + 3 + 3 5 times 3 15 in all	5 + 5 2 times 5 10 in all
2 + 2 + 2 + 2 4 times 2 8 in all	2 + 2 + 2 3 times 2 6 in all	4 + 4 + 4 3 times 4 12 in all

To win, be the first player who gets 3 rectangles with connected sides. Look for these ways to win.

Try Again Play again!

Cover Three

Partner Talk

Share your thinking while you work.

Start 👫 Put  3 4 5 6 in a 🛍.

Get 10 red squares. Get 10 blue squares.
Take turns with another player.

Try Pick 2 tiles. Put them in the blank squares.
Explain how to find the number of
oranges in all.

baskets

If you see the multiplication sentence,
complete it and cover it.

oranges
in each basket

If not, lose your turn.

Put the tiles back in the 🛍.

How many oranges in all?

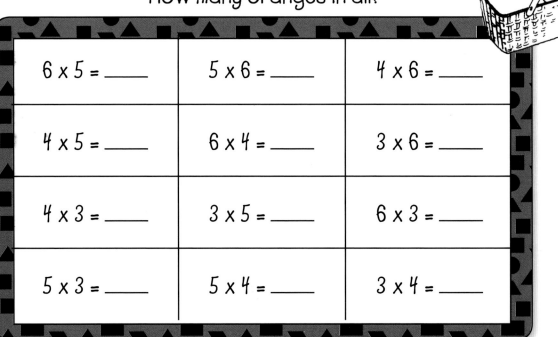

6 x 5 = _____	5 x 6 = _____	4 x 6 = _____
4 x 5 = _____	6 x 4 = _____	3 x 6 = _____
4 x 3 = _____	3 x 5 = _____	6 x 3 = _____
5 x 3 = _____	5 x 4 = _____	3 x 4 = _____

To win, be the first player who gets 3 rectangles with connected sides.
Look for these ways to win.

Try Again Play again!

Helping Hands

Start 👥 Get one 🎲. Get 12 red squares. Take turns.

Try Toss the 🎲. Follow the directions.
Put squares on the workmat. Make an array.

⚀	2 rows 2 squares in each row		⚂	3 rows 3 squares in each row
⚁	3 rows 4 squares in each row		⚃	6 rows 2 squares in each row
⚁	2 rows 5 squares in each row		⚅	3 rows 2 squares in each row

$3 \times 2 = 6$

$2 \times 2 = 4$

$6 \times 2 = 12$

$3 \times 3 = 9$

$3 \times 4 = 12$

$2 \times 5 = 10$

Ask your partner to point
to and say the
multiplication sentence
for your array.

Workmat

Try Again This time, say a repeated addition sentence
before you say the multiplication sentence.

Helping Hands

Partner Talk
Share your thinking while you work.

Start 👥 Get 15 red squares. Get 20 blue squares. Take turns.

Try Choose a multiplication sentence. Do not tell your partner which one. Put blue squares on the workmat. Make the array for your multiplication sentence. Ask your partner to say your multiplication sentence. Cover it with a red square.
Repeat until every multiplication sentence is covered.

$4 \times 4 = 16$

$2 \times 4 = 8$

$5 \times 3 = 15$

$3 \times 2 = 6$

$6 \times 3 = 18$

$4 \times 2 = 8$

$3 \times 4 = 12$

$3 \times 6 = 18$

$3 \times 3 = 9$

Workmat

$1 \times 5 = 5$ $4 \times 3 = 12$ $2 \times 3 = 6$

$3 \times 5 = 15$ $5 \times 2 = 10$ $2 \times 5 = 10$

Try Again This time, point to a multiplication sentence.
Ask your partner to show the array for it.

Partner Talk
Share your thinking while you work.

 Start Put  1 2 3 4 5 in a .

Get 20 red squares. Work together.

Try Pick two tiles from the 🛍. Place them in the blank spaces in the story. Read the story. Use your squares to make an array on your workmat.

Farmer Fred planted sunflower seeds.

He planted ☐ rows with ☐ sunflower seeds

in each row. How many sunflower seeds did Farmer Fred plant?

Display squares on the workmat to act out the story.

Workmat

Say: _____ x _____ = _____

Try Again Put the tiles back in the 🛍. Keep playing! Make five or more stories.

Try Together

Start Get 1 2 3 4 5 6 7 8 9.

Get 20 red squares. Get a . Work together.

Try Read the story. Decide how you want the story to end.
Put a ⬭ below your choice. Then put number tiles in the story
to get that ending. Repeat until you use every ending.

Patty went to the post office to buy stamps.

She got ⬜ rows of stamps with ⬜ stamps

in each row.

CHOOSE THE END OF THE STORY.

Patty bought 18 stamps.
⬭

Patty bought 12 stamps.
⬭

Patty bought 20 stamps.
⬭

Patty bought 16 stamps.
⬭

Patty bought 15 stamps.
⬭

Patty bought 8 stamps.
⬭

Patty bought 14 stamps.
⬭

Patty bought 10 stamps.
⬭

Try Again This time, make two stories for every ending.

Try Together

Partner Talk

Share your thinking while you work.

Start 🚶 Get **2 2 3 3 4 4 5 5**.

Get 12 red squares. Take turns.

Try Show 2 tiles here.

☐ × ☐ = _____

groups   in each group   product

Explain how to find the product. Point to the product below if you see it. Show the same factors next to the chart. Cover the product if it is not already covered. Repeat until every product is covered.

The Product

8	15	12
10	20	6
12	10	8
6	15	20

☐ in each group

× ☐ groups

_____

_____ product

Try Again This time, begin by placing tiles next to the chart. Then show the same factors above the chart.

Partner Talk

Share your thinking while you work.

Try Together

Start  Get ③ ③ ④ ④ ⑤ ⑤ ⑥ ⑥.

Get 12 red squares. Take turns.

Try Point to a product.
Show two factors for that product next to the chart.

The Product

30	20	15
12	24	18
18	20	12
24	15	30

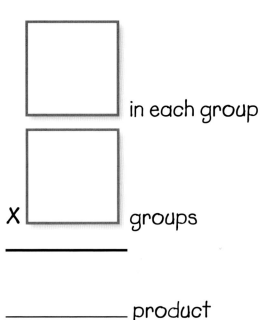

☐ in each group

× ☐ groups
_____

_____ product

Ask your partner to explain why your factors have the product you chose. Display your factors here.

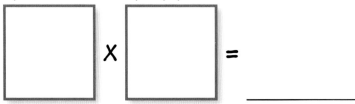

☐ × ☐ = _____
groups   in each group   product

Say the multiplication sentence. Cover the product.
Repeat until every product is covered.

Try Again This time, show the factors below the chart first.
Then move them to the right of the chart.

8 Topic 19 Center Activity 19-4 ★ ★

Try Together

Start 🚶 Get 18 red squares. Take turns.

Try Choose a patio. Fill the patio with squares. Start with the top row. Tell your partner how many squares fit on the patio. Remove your squares. Turn the page sideways. Ask your partner to fill the same patio. Did your partner use the same number of squares?

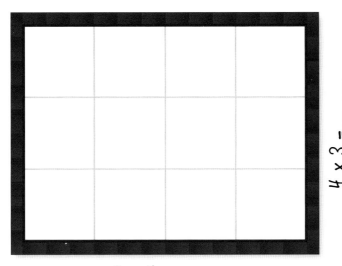

4 x 3 = _____

3 x 4 = _____

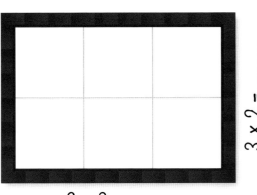

3 x 2 = _____

2 x 3 = _____

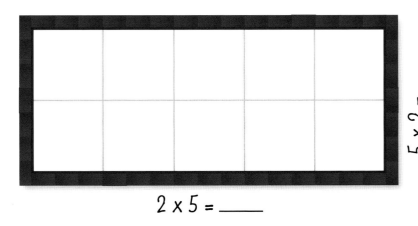

5 x 2 = _____

2 x 5 = _____

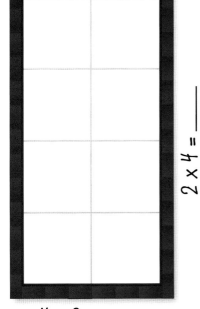

2 x 4 = _____

4 x 2 = _____

Try Again Try every patio. Talk about why the product does not change if the order of the factors changes.

Try Together

Start 👫 Get 6 blue squares to cover the circles.
Get 12 red squares. Take turns.

Try Uncover a circle. Look at the factors. Match them with two gardens that have flowers planted in rows and columns.
Put a red square next to each of those two gardens.
Point to and say a multiplication fact that shows
how many flowers are growing in each garden.

| 3, 4 | 2, 5 | 2, 3 | 4, 2 | 3, 5 | 4, 1 |

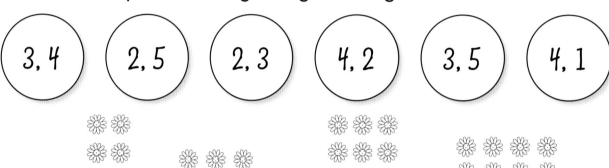

2 x 3 = 6   5 x 3 = 15   2 x 5 = 10
3 x 2 = 6   3 x 5 = 15   5 x 2 = 10

　　　　4 x 3 = 12   4 x 1 = 4   2 x 4 = 8
　　　　3 x 4 = 12   1 x 4 = 4   4 x 2 = 8

Try Again Talk about why the product does not change
if the order of the factors changes.

Look and See

Partner Talk
Share your thinking while you work.

Start 🚶 Get
and .

Get 20 squares. Take turns.

Try Point to a problem. Read it. Put squares on each picture to solve the problem. Then, use tiles to show a multiplication sentence for your picture.

a. There are 3 boxes. Each box has 5 teddy bears. How many teddy bears are there in all?

b. There are 3 boxes. Each box has 2 toy cars. How many toy cars are there in all?

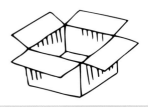 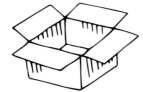 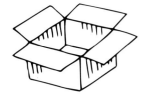

 **X** **=**

c. There are 4 bags. Each bag has 5 marbles. How many marbles are there in all?

d. There are 4 bags. Each bag has three apples. How many apples are there in all?

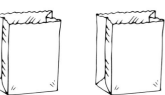 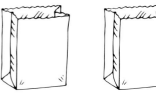

Try Again This time, make up your own problem for each picture. How do pictures help you solve multiplication problems?

Look and See

Start 👥 Get  and .

Get one 🎲. Get 24 squares. Take turns.

Try Point to a problem. Toss the 🎲. Fill the blank line with the number on the 🎲. Read the problem. Put squares on each picture to solve the problem. Use tiles. Show a multiplication sentence for your picture. Take turns until each player gets 6 turns.

a. There are 3 fences. There are _____ flowers growing in front of each fence. How many flowers are growing in front of the fences?

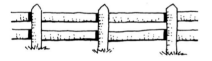 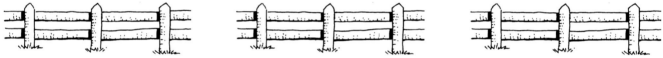 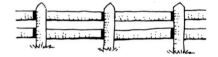

b. There are 4 purses. There are _____ pennies in each purse. How many pennies are in all the purses?

c. There are 2 watermelons. Each watermelon has _____ seeds. How many seeds are there altogether?

Try Again Play again! Talk about how you solve each problem.

Math in Motion

Start Get a . Get 18 red squares. Work together.

Try Pick a number of toys. Put a below it.
Get that number of squares. Pretend your squares are toys.
Share them equally among the 3 toy boxes.

6 balls   9 blocks   3 horns   15 yo-yos

12 jacks   18 rings

Say this sentence to show what happened.

"Each box has _____ _____."

                      Number   Toy Name

Try Again Which toys could you divide equally if you had
only two toy boxes?

Math in Motion

Share your thinking while you work.

Start  Get 20 red squares. Get a ⬭.

Get ⬚1 ⬚2 ⬚3 ⬚4 ⬚5 . Work together.

Try You are making vegetable soup in four pots. Pick a vegetable. Place a ⬭ below it. Then get squares to divide those vegetables among the 4 pots. Put the same number of vegetables in each pot.

16 potatoes

20 beans

4 onions

12 carrots

8 tomatoes

Use a number tile to show the number in each pot.

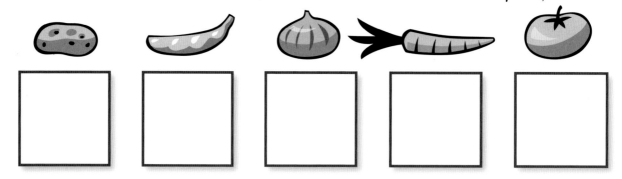

Try Again This time, use only 3 pots. Divide 15 potatoes, 6 beans, 3 onions, 12 carrots and 9 tomatoes.

Try Together

Start 👫 Get 16 red squares. Get ⬭ ⬭ ⬭ ⬭.
Work together.

Try Help the librarian. Pretend that your squares are books.
Point to a note. Follow the directions. Each time you put books
on a shelf, put a ⬭ below a subtraction sentence
to show what you did.

SCHOOL LIBRARY

New Books

Get 16 books. Put 4 on each shelf.

Get 12 books. Put 3 on each shelf.

$12 - 3 = 9$ $4 - 4 = 0$ $9 - 3 = 6$ $16 - 4 = 12$

$6 - 3 = 3$ $12 - 4 = 8$ $8 - 4 = 4$ $3 - 3 = 0$

Try Again This time, tell how many shelves you would need
if you put 2 books on each shelf.

Center Activity 20-2 ⭐

Try Together

Partner Talk
Share your thinking while you work.

Start 👥 Get

and .

Get 18 red squares. Work together.

Try Point to a stack of papers. Get that number of squares. Pretend your squares are pieces of paper. Tell how many desks can get papers if you put 3 pieces of paper on each desk. Each time you put papers on a desk, use number tiles to make a subtraction sentence.

$$\boxed{\qquad} - \boxed{\qquad} = \boxed{\qquad}$$

Try Again Start with with 18 papers. Put 2 on each desk. How many desks can get two papers?

Look and See

Partner Talk

Share your thinking while you work.

 **Start** Get a ⬭. Work together.

Try Read a story. Then point to two pictures that go with that story. Tell how to solve it. Then, put a ⬭ below the matching division sentence. Say it.

Mom has 12 cookies. She wants to share them with her 4 children. How many will each child get?

Morgan has 15 teddy bears. She wants to place them on the 3 shelves in her room. How many bears will go on each shelf?

Sue, Pat, and Cam are making paper crowns. They have a package with 9 sparkling gems in it. How many gems can each child get?

$$12 \div 4 = 3$$

$$9 \div 3 = 3$$

$$15 \div 3 = 5$$

 **Try Again** Talk about other numbers of teddy bears that Morgan could display equally on 3 shelves.

Look and See

Start 👥 Get

and 0 1 2 3 4 5 6 7 8 9 .

Take turns.

Try Choose a picture. Tell a division story. Let your partner use number tiles to make a division sentence. Say the division sentence.

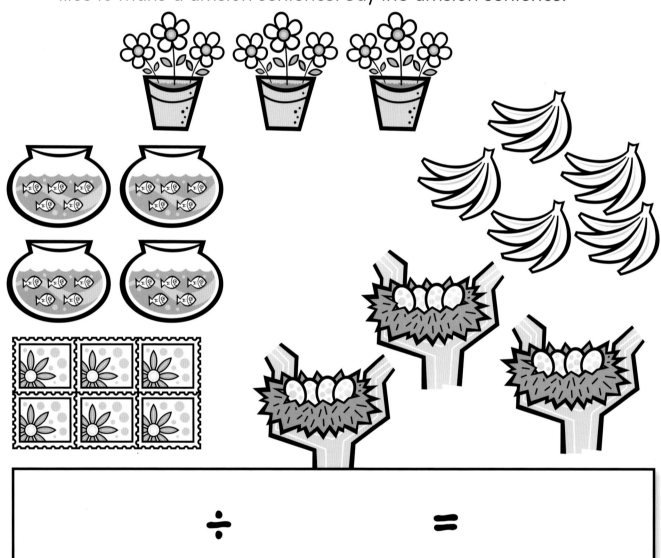

÷ =

Try Again This time, divide in a different way. First, show the number in all. Then show the number of groups, or the number in each group.

Helping Hands

Start 👫 Get 20 red squares. Work together.

Try Look at the garden. Pick a set of flowers. Make an array for them with squares. Let your partner point to a division sentence and a multiplication sentence for your array. Say each number sentence.

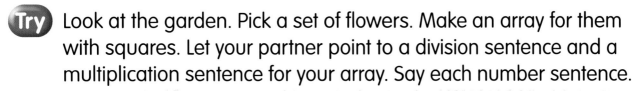

$12 \div 3 = 4$	$4 \times 4 = 16$	$2 \times 6 = 12$	$16 \div 2 = 8$	$10 \div 5 = 2$
$10 \div 2 = 5$	$4 \div 2 = 2$	$5 \times 2 = 10$	$8 \div 4 = 2$	$4 \times 3 = 12$
$8 \times 2 = 16$	$3 \times 4 = 12$	$1 \times 8 = 8$	$4 \times 1 = 4$	$16 \div 4 = 4$
$6 \times 2 = 12$	$12 \div 4 = 3$	$2 \times 2 = 4$	$2 \times 8 = 16$	$2 \times 4 = 8$
$1 \times 4 = 4$	$8 \div 8 = 1$	$4 \times 2 = 8$	$12 \div 6 = 2$	$4 \div 1 = 4$

Try Again This time, make a different array for each set of flowers.

Helping Hands

Start Get
and 0 1 2 3 4 5 6 7 8 9 .

Get 20 red squares. Work together.

Try Pick any number of objects from the art room.
Use squares to show the objects in an array.

15    12   14 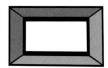   18 ▭   8

Use tiles to make a division sentence and a
multiplication sentence for your array.

÷	=

X	=

Try Again This time, make a different array for each number of objects.

Listen and Learn

Partner Talk
Share your thinking while you work.

Start Get 1 2 3 4 5 6 7 8 9.

Work together.

Try Choose a table. Talk about the pattern. Use number tiles to complete the table. Then read and answer the questions below the table.

Number of Boxes	Number of Toys
1	3
2	
	9
4	12
5	15

a. How many toys are there in 2 boxes?

b. How many boxes would you need to have 18 toys?

Number of Bags	Number of Apples
1	
2	4
3	6
4	
5	10

c. How many apples are there in 4 bags?

d. How many bags do you need for 14 apples?

Number of Bags	Number of Marbles
1	
2	8
3	12
4	16
	20

e. If you have 20 marbles, how many bags are there?

f. How many marbles are there in 10 bags?

Try Again This time, make up your own questions.

Listen and Learn

Partner Talk

Share your thinking while you work.

Start 👫 Get 0 1 2 3 4 5 6 7 8 9 .

Get a 🎲. Work together.

Try Choose a table. Toss the 🎲. Place it on the input side. Show the output with tiles on the output side. Repeat 5 times. Then try another table.

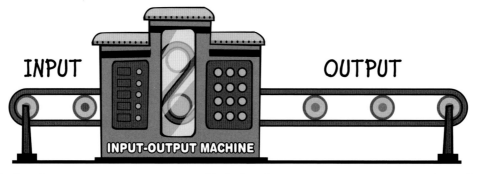

INPUT   OUTPUT

INPUT-OUTPUT MACHINE

Table 1

Pairs	Number of Gloves
1	2
2	
3	
4	8
5	
6	12

a. How many gloves are in 3 pairs?

b. If you have 20 gloves, how many pairs is that?

Table 2

Bags	Number of Apples
1	5
2	
3	
4	20
5	
6	30

c. How many bags of apples do you need for 25 children?

d. If you have 40 apples, how many bags do you have?

Table 3

Cars	Number of Wheels
1	4
2	
3	12
4	
5	
6	24

e. How many wheels are there on 8 cars?

f. How many wheels are on 11 cars?

Try Again This time, answer each question below the table.